Contents Guide

Section 1: Essential Foundations

1. Building Blocks: Prerequisites for Success
2. Navigating the Course: Clear Objectives Ahead
3. Crafting Your Space: Establishing the Development Environment

Section 2: Unveiling Airflow

4. Unraveling Airflow: Unveiling its Power
5. Decoding Airflow: Understanding its Essence
6. Heart of the Engine: Exploring Core Components
7. Mastering the Concepts: Grasping Key Principles
8. Single Node Unveiled: Delving into Singular Architectures
9. Embracing Complexity: Understanding Multi-Node Architectures
10. Behind the Scenes: Unveiling the Inner Workings
11. Setting Sail: Installation Guide for Apache Airflow
12. Docker Demystified: Navigating Containerization
13. Orchestrating with Ease: The Art of docker-compose

Section 3: User Interface Deep Dive

14. Navigating the Dashboard: Exploring DAGs View
15. Setting Sail: Launching Your Maiden DAG
16. A Bird's Eye View: Understanding the Grid Perspective
17. Visualizing Relationships: Embracing the Graph View
18. Timing is Key: Leveraging Landing Times View
19. Marking the Days: Navigating the Calendar View
20. Time in Motion: Unveiling the Gantt View
21. Dive into the Code: Exploring the Code View

Section 4: Crafting Your First Data Pipeline with Airflow

22. Initiating Your Project: A Prelude to Pipeline Creation
23. Setting the Stage: Establishing Your Project Environment
24. Unveiling the DAG: Understanding its Significance
25. Framework Foundations: Building the DAG Skeleton
26. Operator Insights: Deciphering their Role
27. Navigating Providers: Choosing the Right Tools
28. Blueprint for Data: Creating Tables with Precision
29. Establishing Connections: Bridging Data Sources
30. Executing Tasks: Implementing Table Creation
31. Sensor Sensibility: Detecting Data Availability
32. Assessing Availability: Checking API Access
33. Sensing Success: Implementing API Availability Sensor

34. Data Extraction Essentials: Retrieving User Data
35. Extracting Wisdom: Implementing User Extraction
36. User Processing: Transforming Data for Insight
37. Preparing for Execution: Prerequisites for User Processing
38. Processing Prowess: Implementing User Processing
39. Hooking into Data: Understanding their Functionality
40. Data Storage Strategies: Saving User Data
41. Storing Success: Implementing User Storage
42. Sequencing Matters: Ensuring Workflow Integrity
43. Dynamic DAG Dynamics: Witnessing Your DAG in Motion
44. Scheduling Savvy: Mastering DAG Timing
45. Filling the Gaps: Navigating Backfilling Techniques

Section 5: Revolutionizing DAG Scheduling

46. Embracing Evolution: Understanding the Need for Innovation
47. Data Dynamics: Unveiling the Significance of Datasets
48. Farewell to Routine: Rethinking Schedule Intervals
49. Crafting the Producer DAG: Empowering Data Generation
50. Crafting the Consumer DAG: Driving Data Consumption
51. Tracking Tranquility: Leveraging the New View for Dataset Management
52. Patience is a Virtue: Navigating Multi-Dataset Wait Strategies

Section 6: Database Dynamics and Execution Excellence

53. Executor Essentials: Deciphering their Role in Execution
54. Configuration Chronicles: Unveiling Default Settings
55. Sequential Strategy: Understanding the Sequential Executor
56. Local Logic: Harnessing the Power of the Local Executor
57. Celery Charm: Exploring the Celery Executor
58. Config Clarity: Navigating Current Configuration
59. Parallel Prowess: Adding Parallel DAGs to Your Repository
60. Task Transparency: Monitoring Tasks with Flower
61. Streamlining: Removing Default DAG Examples
62. Worker Wonders: Running Tasks on Celery Workers
63. Queue Queries: Understanding the Essence of Queues
64. Expanding Capacity: Adding a New Celery Worker
65. Queue Management: Optimizing Task Distribution
66. Targeted Tasks: Directing Tasks to Specific Queues
67. Concurrency Concepts: Mastering Crucial Parameters for Efficiency

Section 7: Mastering Advanced Airflow Techniques

68. Bidding Farewell to Repetitive Patterns: Streamlining Workflow Structures
69. Introducing Group Dynamics: Incorporating DAG Grouping for Efficiency
70. SubDAG Simplified: Harnessing the Power of SubDAGs
71. Task Grouping Unleashed: Optimizing Workflows with SubDAGs
72. Evolving Strategies: Transitioning from SubDAGs to TaskGroups

73. Task Collaboration: Maximizing Efficiency with TaskGroups
74. Embracing Data Exchange: Adding XCom DAG Functionality
75. Data Dialogue: Facilitating Task Communication with XComs
76. XComs in Motion: Witnessing Data Sharing in Action
77. Directing the Flow: Navigating Conditional Path Execution
78. Conditional Execution: Executing Tasks Based on Conditions
79. Triggering Transformation: Understanding Task Trigger Rules
80. Rule Refinement: Enhancing BranchPythonOperator with Trigger Rules

Section 8: Crafting Airflow Plugins with Elasticsearch and PostgreSQL

81. Prelude to Plugin Power: Introduction to Airflow Plugin Development
82. Exploring Elasticsearch: Unveiling its Significance in Data Management
83. Airflow and Elasticsearch Integration: Configuring Elasticsearch for Airflow
84. Unveiling the Plugin Paradigm: Understanding the Plugin Architecture
85. Establishing Connections: Configuring Connections for Elasticsearch
86. ElasticHook Essentials: Implementing the ElasticHook
87. Plugin Integration: Incorporating ElasticHook into the Plugin Ecosystem
88. Hook Harmony: Witnessing the ElasticHook in Action

~ *Conclusion*

Section 1:
Essential Foundations

Building Blocks: Prerequisites for Success

Before diving headlong into the mechanics of Apache Airflow, it's essential to lay a strong foundation for your journey. In this chapter, we'll establish the key components necessary to ensure your successful use of Apache Airflow for building robust data pipelines.

Core Programming Concepts

- **Python Fundamentals:** Apache Airflow is built in Python. A solid understanding of Python syntax, data structures (lists, dictionaries, tuples), control flow (if/else statements, loops), and object-oriented programming principles will significantly enhance your ability to write and comprehend Airflow DAGs.
    - **Resources:**
        - "Learn Python" Codecademy course: [https://www.codecademy.com/learn/learn-python-3]
        - Official Python Tutorial: [https://docs.python.org/3/tutorial/]
- **Basic Linux Commands:** Airflow deployments often involve Linux environments. Comfort with basic navigation, file manipulation, and permission management in a Linux terminal will prove valuable.
    - **Resources:**
        - "The Linux Command Line" (free book): [https://linuxcommand.org/tlcl.php]
        - Interactive Bash Tutorial: [http://linuxcommand.org/lc3_learning_the_shell.php]

Data Engineering Foundations

- **Understanding ETL:** Extract, Transform, Load (ETL) processes are the backbone of data pipelines. Familiarity with common ETL concepts and tools will help you architect effective workflows within Airflow.
    - **Resources:**

- - Overview of ETL (Wikipedia): [https://en.wikipedia.org/wiki/Extract,_transform,_load]
    - ETL Tools: https://www.capterra.com/extract-transform-load-software/
  - **Databases and SQL:** A working knowledge of relational databases (e.g., PostgreSQL, MySQL) and SQL is often required for interacting with data sources and destinations during your Airflow pipelines.
    - **Resources:**
      - SQLBolt (Interactive SQL Tutorial): [https://sqlbolt.com/]
      - Khan Academy SQL Course: [https://www.khanacademy.org/computing/computer-programming/sql]

Environment and Dependencies

- **Virtual Environments:** Python virtual environments isolate project dependencies from other Python projects. Learn how to create and manage virtual environments using tools like venv or virtualenv.
  - **Resources:**
    - Python Virtual Environments Primer: [https://realpython.com/python-virtual-environments-a-primer/]
- **Package Management (pip):** Understand how to install Airflow and its dependencies using Python's package manager, pip.
  - **Resources:**
    - pip User Guide: [https://pip.pypa.io/en/stable/user_guide/]
- **Version Control (Git):** Using version control like Git allows you to track changes, collaborate effectively, and revert to previous states if needed.
  - **Resources:**
    - "Learn Git in 15 Minutes" Tutorial: [https://www.atlassian.com/git/tutorials/learn-git-with-bitbucket-cloud]

Cloud Concepts (Optional but Beneficial)

- **Cloud Providers:** Airflow can be deployed in cloud environments like AWS, Azure, or GCP. A basic familiarity with cloud service concepts will be helpful, especially if you plan to deploy Airflow in production.
  - **Resources:**
    - Cloud Computing Basics: [https://azure.microsoft.com/en-us/overview/what-is-cloud-computing/]

Let's Get Practical

To start putting this knowledge into action, try these exercises:

1. **Install Python:** Get Python up and running on your system.
2. **Python Basics Practice:** Complete a few beginner Python tutorials.
3. **Linux Exploration:** Experiment with a Linux virtual machine or environment.
4. **Database Basics:** Set up a simple local database (e.g., SQLite) and try SQL queries.

Remember, a robust foundation today will pave the way for a smooth and successful Apache Airflow implementation tomorrow!

Navigating the Course: Clear Objectives Ahead

Before you embark on your Airflow adventure, it's vital to chart a clear course by defining precise objectives. This chapter sets you up for success by helping you:

- **Understand the 'Why:'** Identify core reasons for adopting Apache Airflow in your workflow automation arsenal.
- **Set Realistic Goals:** Outline specific outcomes you aim to achieve using Airflow.
- **Map Your Data Landscape:** Identify data sources, destinations, and the pipelines needed to connect them.

Why Apache Airflow?

Start by reflecting on the following questions to solidify your motivation for choosing Airflow:

- **Current Pain Points:** What are the bottlenecks or inefficiencies in your existing data management processes? Does Airflow address these?
    - Examples: Manual workflows, error-prone pipelines, lack of visibility, scheduling difficulties.
- **Desired Capabilities:** What key features of Airflow align with your needs?
    - Examples: Dynamic workflows, scalability, robust monitoring, open-source ecosystem.
- **Data Workflow Complexity:** Is your workflow intricate enough to warrant Airflow's capabilities, or would a simpler scripting solution suffice?
- **Team Skills:** Does your team have the Python and data engineering skills for Airflow? Or are you prepared to invest in learning?

Setting Achievable Goals

Once you understand the 'why,' break down your broad vision into specific, measurable goals. Consider these aspects:

- **Specific Use Cases:** Pinpoint the first few data pipelines you'll build with Airflow. Focus on well-defined problems.
    - Examples: Automate report generation, streamline data ingestion for a machine learning model, orchestrate database cleanup.
- **Scheduling:** How often do you need these pipelines to run? Daily? Hourly? Based on external triggers?
- **Scalability Goals:** What's the anticipated data volume increase over time? Can Airflow handle your projected future needs?

- **Monitoring Requirements:** What metrics are essential to track pipeline health? Airflow execution time, failed tasks, resource usage?

Mapping Your Data Landscape

Visualize the flow of data by answering these questions:

- **Internal Sources:** Which databases, applications, or file systems will Airflow need to pull data from?
- **External Sources:** Will you integrate with cloud storage, 3rd-party APIs, or streaming services?
- **Data Transformations:** What kind of data cleaning, aggregation, or modeling will occur within your Airflow pipelines?
- **Destinations:** Where will the processed data ultimately be stored or used? Databases, visualization tools, machine learning models?

Example: A Small Business Scenario

Let's say a small e-commerce business wants to use Airflow for:

- **Why:** Replace manual sales report generation and customer data updates.
- **Goals:**
    - Generate daily sales reports by 7 AM EST.
    - Update a CRM system with new customer information every hour.
- **Data Landscape:**
    - **Sources:** MySQL database (orders), Google Sheets (marketing leads)
    - **Transformations:** Calculations, filtering of data.
    - **Destinations:** Dashboarding tool, CRM system.

Practical Exercise

1. **Brainstorm:** List 3-5 problems Airflow could address in *your* workflow.
2. **Define Goals:** For each problem, outline 2-3 specific objectives.
3. **Sketch your Data Map:** Draw a simple diagram of your data sources, transformations, and destinations.

Keep Evolving

As you gain experience, you'll reevaluate these objectives and set more advanced ones. Remember, clarity here will guide your successful exploration of Airflow!

Additional Resources

- **Apache Airflow Documentation:** https://airflow.apache.org/docs/]
- **Common Data Workflow Scenarios:** https://towardsdatascience.com/common-data-workflow-scenarios-and-tools-82a6b52c3b31

Crafting Your Space: Establishing the Development Environment

Before embarking on building Airflow pipelines, it's vital to set up a comfortable and functional development environment. Think of it as your workshop – a space where you'll experiment, build, and refine your workflows. This chapter will guide you through the essentials:

1. Choosing Your Playground

- **Local Development:**
    - Suited for: Experimentation, learning, small-scale setups.
    - Pros: Quick setup, full control.
    - Cons: Can differ from production environments, potential resource limitations.
- **Cloud-Based Development:**
    - Suited for: Larger projects, closer resemblance to production setups, remote collaboration.
    - Pros: Scalability, potential for faster setup with managed Airflow services.
    - Cons: May incur costs, requires familiarity with cloud platforms.

2. Essential Tools

- **Text Editor / IDE:** Choose your weapon for writing Python code:
    - Beginners: VS Code (https://code.visualstudio.com/), Atom (https://atom.io/), PyCharm Community Edition (https://www.jetbrains.com/pycharm/).
    - More Experienced: Vim (https://www.vim.org/), Emacs (https://www.gnu.org/software/emacs/), PyCharm Professional Edition.
- **Version Control (Git):** Track changes, experiment, and collaborate seamlessly. Install Git locally (https://git-scm.com/).
- **Virtual Environment Tool:** Options include `venv` or `virtualenv` – learn their use for managing dependencies.

3. Installing Apache Airflow

- **Core Installation:** Use `pip install apache-airflow` for the base Airflow package.
- **Providers:** Install provider packages for specific integrations
    - Examples: `pip install apache-airflow-providers-amazon`, `pip install apache-airflow-providers-google`

- **Constraints File (Optional):** Consider a constraints file to manage dependency conflicts, especially in larger projects. Learn the format at [invalid URL removed]]

4. Setting the Stage: The AIRFLOW_HOME Directory

- **Purpose:** Airflow stores configuration files, your DAGs, and logs in a designated folder – AIRFLOW_HOME.
- **Default:** Usually ~/airflow (modify as needed).
- **Creation:** The Airflow installer should create it automatically. If not, create the directory manually.

5. Test Flight: Your First DAG Execution

- **Airflow Initialization:** `airflow db init` sets up the metadata database.
- **Starting the Engine:**
    - `airflow webserver` launches the Airflow web interface.
    - `airflow scheduler` starts the Airflow scheduler.
- **Accessing the Web Interface:** Usually via `http://localhost:8080`: http://localhost:8080 in your browser.

Environment Variations

- **Docker:** Containerize your environment for consistency. Explore Airflow's official Docker image (https://airflow.apache.org/docs/docker-stack/index.html]).
- **Cloud Providers:** AWS, Azure, and GCP offer managed Airflow services to simplify setup and scaling.

Practical Tips

- **Begin with a Basic Local Setup:** Start learning Airflow on your own machine.
- **Document Your Setup:** Note versions, providers, custom settings for future reference.
- **Consider a Project Template:** Create a standard folder structure for DAGs, configuration files, and logs.

Additional Resources

- **Airflow Installation Guide:** https://airflow.apache.org/docs/apache-airflow/stable/installation/index.html]
- **Virtual Environment Primer:** https://realpython.com/python-virtual-environments-a-primer/]

Section 2:
Unveiling Airflow

Unraveling Airflow: Unveiling its Power

In the realm of data workflow automation, Apache Airflow reigns supreme. This chapter initiates your journey into understanding why Airflow has become such a force to be reckoned with. We'll unravel the core advantages it offers, scenarios where it excels, and the reasons behind its widespread adoption.

The Airflow Advantage

- **Dynamic Pipeline Creation:** Airflow empowers you to define complex workflows as code using Python. Gone are the days of rigid, static pipelines!
- **Rich Functionality:** Operators, sensors, hooks, and a powerful scheduling engine form Airflow's potent toolkit for constructing diverse data pipelines.
- **Scalability:** Airflow can scale from modest setups to distributed systems, gracefully handling growing data volumes and workload complexities.
- **Extensible Architecture:** The plugin framework lets you integrate seamlessly with a vast range of external tools and data sources.
- **Vibrant Community:** A thriving community of users and developers provides support, shares knowledge, and drives Airflow's continuous improvement.

Airflow in Action: When to Choose It

Airflow stands out in the following scenarios:

- **Complex Workflows:** When you need to orchestrate intricate sequences of tasks with dependencies and conditional logic, Airflow shines.
- **Frequent Scheduling:** Airflow excels at running data pipelines on precise schedules – hourly, daily, weekly, or even more frequently.
- **Data from Diverse Sources:** Integrate disparate data sources like databases, cloud services, APIs, and flat files with Airflow's vast provider library.
- **Workflow Monitoring and Visibility:** Airflow's intuitive UI provides a real-time window into pipeline health and progress.
- **Re-running and Backfilling Tasks:** Easily correct errors by re-running failed tasks or backfilling missing data from past execution intervals.

Limitations to Consider

Like any powerful tool, Airflow also has a few considerations:

- **Learning Curve:** Mastering Airflow involves programming concepts and an understanding of its components.
- **Real-time Streaming:** Airflow is better suited for batch processing than continuous, real-time streaming.
- **Setup:** Deploying a production-grade Airflow environment can involve moderate complexity.

Real-World Use Cases

The versatility of Airflow is evident in its wide range of applications:

- **Data Engineering:** Building ETL pipelines for data ingestion, cleaning, and transformation.
- **Machine Learning Pipelines:** Automating model training, deployment, and monitoring.
- **Reporting and Analytics:** Generating regular business intelligence reports or dashboards.
- **Infrastructure Automation:** Orchestrating infrastructure tasks such as backups or updates.
- **Scientific Workflows:** Managing and automating complex sequences in scientific computations.

Why Airflow? A Quick Recap

1. **Programmatic Workflows:** Python grants you control and flexibility.
2. **Diverse Toolset:** Operators, sensors, and hooks form a versatile arsenal.
3. **Made to Scale:** Accommodates large-scale data processing seamlessly.
4. **Customizability:** Plugins open a world of integrations.
5. **Strong Support:** Backed by a passionate open-source community.

Let's Get Practical

- **Think of a Problem:** Identify a repetitive, multi-step data task you currently handle manually. Could Airflow automate it?

Additional Resources

- **Airflow Documentation (Concepts):**
  https://airflow.apache.org/docs/apache-airflow/stable/concepts.html
- **Real-World Airflow Use Cases:**
  https://www.astronomer.io/blog/airflow-use-cases

The next chapter will delve deeper as we begin "Decoding Airflow: Understanding its Essence."

Decoding Airflow: Understanding its Essence

In the previous chapter, we caught a glimpse of Airflow's power. Now, let's decode the fundamental building blocks and concepts that make Airflow tick. Think of this as cracking open the machine to see how the gears turn.

Key Components: The Building Blocks

- **DAGs (Directed Acyclic Graphs):** The heart of Airflow. DAGs are blueprints that define the structure of your workflows – the tasks involved, their dependencies, and execution order. Written in Python, they provide immense flexibility.
- **Operators:** The workhorses of your DAG. These self-contained units of logic represent individual tasks within your workflow. Airflow provides built-in operators (e.g., `BashOperator`, `PythonOperator`, `EmailOperator`) and the ability to create custom ones if needed.
- **Tasks:** Instances of operators within a DAG. Each task represents a single, concrete step in your workflow.
- **Scheduler:** The tireless timekeeper. Airflow's scheduler orchestrates your DAGs' execution based on their schedule intervals or external triggers.
- **Executor:** The conductor that determines how tasks are ultimately carried out. Airflow supports different executors like the `SequentialExecutor`, `LocalExecutor`, and `CeleryExecutor` for various scaling needs.
- **Web Server:** The command center. Airflow's web interface provides a dashboard for monitoring your DAGs, task statuses, logs, and more.

Core Concepts: Mastering the Vocabulary

- **Schedule Intervals:** Define how often a DAG should run. These can be specified using cron expressions or human-readable intervals like `@daily` or `@weekly`.
- **Dependencies:** The relationships between tasks. Airflow excels at orchestrating complex workflows by ensuring tasks run in the correct order based on their dependencies.
- **Upstream and Downstream:** Tasks positioned earlier in the workflow are "upstream," while those positioned later are "downstream." Dependencies flow from upstream to downstream tasks.
- **Metadata Database:** Airflow's "brain" where it stores information about your DAGs, task statuses, logs, and past historical runs.

Workflow as Code

Airflow's philosophy of representing workflows as Python code empowers you with:

- **Version Control:** Track changes to your workflows using tools like Git.
- **Dynamic Logic:** Introduce conditional branching, loops, and variables for adaptable pipelines.
- **Reusability:** Share common patterns between DAGs through functions or custom operators.

Understanding Airflow Architecture

At a high level, Airflow's key components collaborate in a harmonious cycle:

1. **DAG Parsing:** The Scheduler periodically scans your AIRFLOW_HOME directory for DAG files.
2. **Scheduling** Loaded DAGs are scheduled for execution by the Scheduler, respecting their timing requirements.
3. **Task Execution:** The chosen Executor distributes tasks to available workers in your environment.
4. **Monitoring:** The Webserver provides a visual interface to track DAG runs and task statuses.
5. **Database Updates:** The Metadata Database persistently records the state of your DAGs and tasks.

Practical Exercise

1. **Visualize a Simple DAG:** Sketch a simple DAG with 3-4 tasks. Draw arrows to indicate dependencies. This helps visualize the core concepts.

Additional Resources

- **Airflow Documentation (Components):**
  https://airflow.apache.org/docs/apache-airflow/stable/concepts/overview.html
- **Understanding Key Airflow Concepts:**
  https://airflow.apache.org/docs/apache-airflow/stable/concepts/index.html

In the next chapter, we'll examine the "Heart of the Engine: Exploring Core Components" – get ready for a deep dive!

Heart of the Engine: Exploring Core Components

In this chapter, we'll examine the vital organs that make up the Airflow system. Get ready to dissect the Scheduler, Executor, Web Server, and Metadata Database – the pillars upon which Airflow's robust operations rest.

1. The Scheduler: Airflow's Timekeeper

- **Purpose:** Ensures your DAGs run according to their defined schedules, continuously checking for DAGs that need execution.
- **Behind the Scenes:**
    - Periodically scans your `AIRFLOW_HOME` for new or modified DAGs.
    - Evaluates schedule intervals (`@hourly`, `0 0 * * *`, etc.).
    - Looks for tasks within DAGs whose start dates have passed and dependencies are met.
    - Creates entries in the Metadata Database to track these tasks ready for execution.
- **Key Role:** Acts as the tireless heartbeat that initiates your workflows.

2. The Executor: Task Orchestrator

- **Purpose:** The conductor responsible for carrying out individual tasks within your DAGs.
- **Flexible Strategies:** Airflow supports different Executors to suit your needs:
    - **SequentialExecutor:** For local development, executes tasks one at a time.
    - **LocalExecutor:** Allows multiple tasks within a single process – good for testing.
    - **CeleryExecutor:** For production, distributes tasks across multiple worker nodes for scaling.
    - **KubernetesExecutor** – Ideal for dynamic and containerized environments.
- **Key Role:** Determines *how* your tasks are ultimately run.

3. The Web Server: Your Visual Control Center

- **Purpose:** Provides a user-friendly, graphical interface for interacting with Airflow.
- **Key Features:**
    - **DAG Overview:** Visualize your DAGs, task statuses (running, failed, success).
    - **Monitoring:** Track progress, run times, and dependencies.

- ○ **Troubleshooting:** Access logs to pinpoint errors.
- ○ **Management:** Triggering DAG runs manually, configuring variables.
- **Key Role:** Your window into the health and progress of your Airflow pipelines.

4. The Metadata Database: Airflow's Memory

- **Purpose:** The brain of Airflow – stores crucial information about your workflows.
- **What It Stores:**
  - ○ DAG definitions
  - ○ Task statuses (past and present)
  - ○ Run history
  - ○ Variables
  - ○ Connections
- **Technologies:** Commonly uses relational databases like PostgreSQL or MySQL.
- **Key Role:** Underpins Airflow's monitoring, scheduling, and execution capabilities.

The Interconnected Ecosystem

Remember, these core components work in perfect concert:

1. **Scheduler:** Determines what tasks need to run.
2. **Executor:** Handles task execution according to your chosen strategy.
3. **Web Server:** Visualizes the state of your system.
4. **Metadata Database:** Persistently stores all the crucial information for seamless operation.

Practical Tip

- **Exploring the Web UI:** Dive into your Airflow installation's web interface. Inspect a default DAG and poke around the UI to understand the layout and functionality.

Additional Resources

- **Airflow Components Documentation:**
  https://airflow.apache.org/docs/apache-airflow/stable/concepts/overview.html
- **Article on Airflow Executors:**
  https://towardsdatascience.com/airflow-executors-explained-44fb485d2b16

In the next chapter, we'll tackle "Mastering the Concepts: Grasping Key Principles" – prepare to build a solid foundation in Airflow fundamentals!

Mastering the Concepts: Grasping Key Principles

Let's solidify those crucial Airflow concepts. Think of this chapter as building a mental toolkit to make your workflow designs efficient and robust.

1. DAGs: The Blueprint

- **Definition:** DAGs (Directed Acyclic Graphs) are the heart of Airflow. Remember, they define the structure (tasks), order (dependencies), and schedule of your workflows.
- **Directed:** Tasks have a clear direction of flow, from upstream to downstream.
- **Acyclic:** No circular dependencies allowed! This ensures your workflows can complete successfully.
- **Written in Python:** This brings flexibility and the power of programming to pipeline design.

2. Tasks: The Action Units

- **Definition:** Tasks are the individual workhorses of your DAG, representing discrete steps in your workflow (e.g., run a SQL query, process a file, trigger an API call).
- **Powered by Operators:** Each task is an instance of a built-in or custom operator that provides the logic for execution.

3. Operators: The Versatile Toolkit

- **Pre-built Powerhouses:** Airflow offers a vast library of operators:
    - `BashOperator` (Execute Bash commands)
    - `PythonOperator` (Run Python functions)
    - `EmailOperator` (Send emails)
    - `PostgresOperator` (Interact with PostgreSQL databases)
    - ...and many more!
- **Provider Packages:** Extend functionality for specific services (e.g., `aws`, `google`, `slack`).
- **Custom Operators:** Build your own when needed, for maximum flexibility.

4. Dependencies: Defining Relationships

- **Mapping the Flow:** Clearly outline how tasks relate using operators like >>, <<, or by calling `.set_upstream()` and `.set_downstream()`.
- **Key Concept:** Ensures tasks run in the correct order and prevents chaos. Upstream tasks *must* complete before downstream tasks begin.

5. Schedule Intervals: When to Run

- **Timetables:** Specify how often a DAG runs using:
  - Human-readable intervals: `@daily`, `@hourly`, `@monthly`
  - Cron expressions: Fine-grained control (e.g., "Run at 5 AM on the first Friday of each month")
- **Triggering:** DAGs can also be triggered by external events.

6. Data Sharing (XComs): Tasks Collaborate

- **The Need:** Often, tasks need to pass information to each other.
- **XComs to the Rescue:** A mechanism for tasks to push and pull small pieces of data (e.g., filenames, status updates, results).
- **Key Concepts:**
  - `xcom_push()` (send data downstream)
  - `xcom_pull()` (retrieve data from upstream)

7. Idempotency: Resilience Matters

- **Definition:** Tasks that produce the same outcome each time they run, even with repeated execution.
- **Why it Matters:**
  - Makes rerunning failed tasks easier.
  - Helps ensure data consistency in your pipelines.

Let's Get Practical

1. **Sketch a DAG:** Draw a simple DAG with dependencies to visualize these concepts.

Additional Resources

- **Apache Airflow Documentation (Concepts):**
  https://airflow.apache.org/docs/apache-airflow/stable/concepts.html
- **Airflow Best Practices:**
  https://airflow.apache.org/docs/apache-airflow/stable/best-practices.html

In the next chapter, we'll delve into "Single Node Unveiled: Delving into Singular Architectures," examining how Airflow works on a single machine.

Single Node Unveiled: Delving into Singular Architectures

Often the best way to grasp complex systems is to start with their simplest form. In this chapter, we'll examine a typical single-node Airflow setup, ideal for development, testing, and smaller-scale pipelines.

The Blueprint: Essential Components

- **Metadata Database:**
    - Stores DAG definitions, task and run history, connections, etc.
    - Commonly uses SQLite (for simple setups) or PostgreSQL/MySQL for heavier usage.
- **Scheduler:**
    - Scans for DAGs, checks dependencies and schedule intervals.
    - Sends tasks ready for execution to the executor.
- **Executor:**
    - The simplest option is the SequentialExecutor. It executes tasks one at a time, within the Scheduler's process itself.
- **Web Server:**
    - Provides the graphical user interface for interacting with your Airflow system.
- **Worker(s):**
    - Technically, the SequentialExecutor uses a single worker process within the Scheduler.

How It All Works Together (Simplified)

1. **DAG Parsing:** The Scheduler continuously looks for new or updated DAGs in your AIRFLOW_HOME folder.
2. **Task Identification:** The Scheduler evaluates each DAG's schedule interval and dependencies to determine tasks that need to run.
3. **Execution (Sequential):** With the SequentialExecutor, tasks are run *one after the other*, directly within the Scheduler process.
4. **Web Interface:** Access the Web Server to visualize DAGs, their statuses, and run historical logs.
5. **Database Updates:** The Metadata Database persistently stores all this information.

Key Points: Single Node

- **All-In-One:** All core components run within a single machine.

- **Sufficiency:** Great for experimentation, learning Airflow, and smaller-scale operations.
- **Limitations:**
  - No inherent parallelism. Tasks execute sequentially.
  - Limited by the resources (CPU, memory) of the single machine.

When Single-Node Shines

- **Development and Prototyping:** Spin up a local Airflow instance quickly.
- **Small Workloads:** When your data pipelines are modest.

When to Scale Up

- **Parallelism:** If you need multiple tasks to run simultaneously.
- **Resource Constraints:** A single machine becomes a bottleneck for large datasets or many DAGs.
- **Reliability:** Single points of failure can bring your whole setup down.

Practical Observation

- Witness the `SequentialExecutor` in action. Set up a simple DAG, and observe in the Airflow UI how tasks execute one after another.

Additional Resources

- **Airflow Executors: Different Deployments**
  https://airflow.apache.org/docs/apache-airflow/stable/executor/index.html
- **Scaling Airflow:**
  https://airflow.apache.org/docs/apache-airflow/stable/production-deployment.html

Next Up: We'll explore how Airflow handles complex, resource-intensive workloads with "Embracing Complexity: Understanding Multi-Node Architectures."

Embracing Complexity: Understanding Multi-Node Architectures

When your data pipelines grow in size and complexity, the humble single-node Airflow setup starts to reach its limits. Enter multi-node architectures, designed to handle greater workloads, parallelism, and increased reliability. Let's break it down.

Why Go Distributed?

- **Breaking the Bottleneck:** Scale beyond the processing power of a single machine.
- **True Parallelism:** Run multiple tasks simultaneously for faster execution.
- **High Availability:** No single point of failure; your Airflow system stays up.
- **Resource Allocation:** Match different workloads with specialized hardware (high memory vs. high CPU).

New Components for Scaling

1. **Celery Executor:**
   - Designed for distributed execution.
   - Introduces new components: Worker Nodes and a Message Broker.
2. **Worker Nodes:** Separate machines (physical or virtual) dedicated to executing tasks.
3. **Message Broker (Celery's Backbone):** Facilitates communication between the Scheduler, workers, and the result backend. Popular choices include:
   - Redis: Lightweight and fast.
   - RabbitMQ: Robust and feature-rich.

How the Architecture Evolves

- **Scheduler:** Still the mastermind, determining *what* needs to run.
- **Web Server:** Your monitoring and control center.
- **Metadata Database:** Holds the collective knowledge.
- **Workers (Celery):** Now on separate nodes, they receive tasks from the Scheduler via the message broker and carry out the work.
- **Message Broker:** The communication highway between the Scheduler and Celery workers.

Workflow in a Distributed Setup

1. **Scheduling:** Scheduler scans for DAGs and determines ready tasks.
2. **Message Queue:** Scheduler sends tasks ready for execution to the message broker.

3. **Work Distribution:** Celery workers pick up available tasks from the message queue.
4. **Execution:** Tasks run on worker nodes.
5. **Results & Updates:** Workers communicate task status and results back through the message broker, which updates the database.

Key Considerations

- **Capacity Planning:** How many worker nodes, and with what resources, to match your workloads?
- **Message Broker:** Choosing the right broker for your reliability and scaling needs.
- **Horizontal Scalability:** Can you easily add more worker nodes as demand grows?
- **Monitoring:** Distributed systems need visibility. Track your workers and message queue health.
- **Experiment:** Spin up a basic Airflow setup using the CeleryExecutor (you can even simulate multiple workers on your local machine). Observe how tasks get distributed.

Additional Resources

- **Airflow Docs: Scaling Out with Celery:**
  https://airflow.apache.org/docs/apache-airflow/stable/executor/celery.html
- **Celery Distributed Task Queue Website:**
  https://docs.celeryq.dev/en/stable/index.html

In the next chapter, "Behind the Scenes: Unveiling the Inner Workings," we'll take a peek under the hood of Airflow's operations!

Behind the Scenes: Unveiling the Inner Workings

In this chapter, we'll go beyond the 'what' and explore the 'how'. Get ready to understand the key processes that drive Airflow's robust operations.

1. The Heartbeat: The Scheduler's Cycle

- **DAG Parsing:** Continuously scans your AIRFLOW_HOME directory:
    - Looks for new DAG files.
    - Detects any modifications made to existing DAGs.
- **Dependency Check:** Analyzes each task within a DAG and its dependencies. Tasks can only be scheduled if their upstream dependencies have been met.
- **Task Evaluation:** Examines schedule intervals (@hourly, etc.). If a task's 'start date' is in the past and dependencies are met, the Scheduler marks it 'ready for execution'.
- **Database Updates:** Persistently writes the state of tasks into the metadata database.

2. Executing Tasks: How Executors Get Things Done

- **The Task Dispatch Process:**
    - Scheduler picks 'ready' tasks from the database.
    - Executor retrieves these tasks and determines how to execute them.
    - **SequentialExecutor:** Runs tasks within the Scheduler process, one-by-one.
    - **LocalExecutor:** Executes tasks in separate processes, allows some parallelism.
    - **CeleryExecutor:** Sends tasks to the message broker for distribution to Celery workers.

3. The Metadata Database: The Brain of the Operation

- **Storehouse of Knowledge:** Holds information about:
    - Your DAG definitions
    - Historical and current task states (running, success, failed, etc.)
    - Schedule intervals
    - Connections to external systems
    - Variables
    - …and much more!
- **Behind-the-Scenes Queries:** Airflow components continuously interact with the database to make scheduling and execution decisions, as well as update statuses.

4. The Web Server: Your Visual Window

- **Serving Views:** Renders the Airflow graphical interface you interact with.
- **Communication Hub:** Fetches live DAG and task information from the Metadata Database to display:
    - DAG run statuses
    - Task logs
    - Gantt charts
    - And more.

5. Monitoring and Logging: Keeping an Eye on Things

- **Task Logs:** Each task's output is captured in logs that you can access via the UI. Crucial for debugging.
- **Web Server Logs:** Records Airflow's own operations.
- **Metadata Database:** Historical data provides a comprehensive record of past runs.
- **Integration Potential:** Airflow can send logs and metrics to external logging/monitoring systems.

Practical Tip

- **Dive into Logs:** When you encounter issues, task and Airflow logs become your troubleshooting best friend.
- **Database Exploration:** Get a feel for the data stored in Airflow's metadata database. You can try querying it directly for a deeper understanding.

Additional Resources

- **Airflow Under the Hood (Article):** https://medium.com/@deepak_67659/airflow-under-the-hood-61a91dab753d
- **Understanding Airflow's Metadata Database:** https://airflow.apache.org/docs/apache-airflow/stable/concepts/execution-date.html#execution-date

Next, let's get hands-on with a "Setting Sail: Installation Guide for Apache Airflow." Let's turn this knowledge into action!

Setting Sail: Installation Guide for Apache Airflow

In this chapter, we'll prepare your environment and install Apache Airflow, transforming your machine into an Airflow command center.

Prerequisites

- **Operating System:** Airflow works well on Linux, macOS, or Windows (via Windows Subsystem for Linux).
- **Python:** Python 3.7 or newer (check with `python --version`).
- **pip:** Python's package installer (`python -m ensurepip --upgrade`).

Step 1: Creating an Airflow Home

- Designate a directory to serve as Airflow's base of operations. This will house your DAGs, configuration files, and logs.
    - Example: `mkdir ~/airflow`

Step 2: Setting up a Virtual Environment (Highly Recommended)

- It's best to isolate Airflow's dependencies to avoid conflicts.
    - `python3 -m venv <environment_name>` (example: `python3 -m venv airflow_env`)
    - `source <environment_name>/bin/activate` (example: `source airflow_env/bin/activate`)

Step 3: Installing Airflow

- The core installation:
    - `pip install apache-airflow`
- **Providers:** Consider installing providers for your specific needs (AWS, Google Cloud, etc.)
    - Example: `pip install apache-airflow-providers-amazon`

Step 4: Initiating the Airflow Environment

- `airflow db init` (This sets up the Metadata Database)

Step 5: Launching Airflow

- Start the Web Server: `airflow webserver`
- Start the Scheduler: `airflow scheduler`

Accessing the Web Interface

- Open a web browser and go to http://localhost:8080. Welcome to Airflow's UI!

Common Installation Scenarios

- **SQLite vs. Production Databases:**
  - For starting out, SQLite is fine. For serious deployments, consider PostgreSQL or MySQL.
- **Choosing an Executor:**
  - Start with `SequentialExecutor` for experimentation. For scaling, explore `CeleryExecutor` or `KubernetesExecutor`.

Troubleshooting Tips

- **Check your Python Version:** Airflow needs the right Python environment.
- **Dependency Issues:** Isolate your Airflow environment with a virtual environment.
- **Documentation is Your Friend:** Refer to the official Airflow installation docs if you get stuck.

Extra Configuration (Optional)

- `airflow.cfg`: Airflow's configuration file resides in your AIRFLOW_HOME. Explore and customize its settings.

Practical Exercise

1. Install Airflow in a fresh virtual environment.
2. Access the Web UI and poke around. Can you find the list of example DAGs?

Additional Resources

- **Airflow Installation Documentation:**
  https://airflow.apache.org/docs/apache-airflow/stable/installation/index.html
- **Managing Airflow Environments:**
  https://www.astronomer.io/guides/managing-airflow-environments

Next Up: We'll explore "Docker Demystified: Navigating Containerization," learning how to streamline your Airflow setup with containers!

Docker Demystified: Navigating Containerization

Often, setting up complex software like Airflow leads to dependency headaches: "It works on my machine, but why not yours?" Enter Docker, designed to make life easier.

1. The Concept of Containers

- **Analogy:** Think of containers like tiny, self-contained boxes. Each box bundles your application (Airflow), its code, dependencies, and even a mini operating system.
- **Benefits:**
    - **Portability:** Run your packaged container anywhere Docker is supported – your laptop, a cloud server, etc.
    - **Consistency:** No more "works on my machine" woes. Environments are identical.
    - **Isolation:** Each container is its own world, preventing conflicts with other things on your system.

2. Docker Basics

- **Docker Image:** The blueprint for your container. It's like a snapshot of everything needed to run your Airflow environment.
- **Docker Container:** A running instance of a Docker image. You can have multiple containers based on the same image.
- **Dockerfile:** A recipe (text file) that defines how your Docker image is built.
- **Docker Hub:** A vast online repository for storing and sharing pre-built Docker images.

3. Airflow and Docker: A Perfect Match

- **Streamlined Setup:** A Docker image can package Airflow with all its exact dependencies.
- **Deployment Heaven:** Move your Dockerized Airflow between development, testing, and production seamlessly.
- **Scaling with Ease:** Spin up multiple Airflow worker containers on-demand using the same image.

4. A Basic Airflow Dockerfile (Example)

```
FROM apache/airflow:2.4.3   # Base Airflow image

COPY requirements.txt /requirements.txt
```

```
RUN pip install -r /requirements.txt   # Install your
requirements

COPY dags/ /opt/airflow/dags   # Add your DAGs

# Any additional configuration here...
```

5. Building and Running

- **Building the Image:** `docker build -t my-airflow-image .` (from the directory containing your Dockerfile)
- **Running a Container:** `docker run -d -p 8080:8080 my-airflow-image` (this exposes Airflow's web interface)

Beyond the Basics

- **Volumes:** Map directories on your machine to directories within the container (to persist your DAGs and logs outside the container itself).
- **Networking:** Link containers for Airflow components (worker, webserver) to communicate.
- **docker-compose:** A powerful tool to orchestrate multi-container setups (we'll cover this in the next chapter!)

Practical Exercise

1. **Find an Airflow Docker Image:** Search on Docker Hub for a base Airflow image.
2. **Write a Simple Dockerfile:** Extend the base image to include a sample DAG of your own.

Additional Resources

- **Docker Intro:** https://www.docker.com/get-started
- **Official Airflow Docker Image:** https://hub.docker.com/r/apache/airflow
- **Docker for Data Science:** https://docs.docker.com/solutions/data-science/

In the next chapter, "Orchestrating with Ease: The Art of docker-compose," we'll see how to manage complex Airflow deployments with multiple components.

Orchestrating with Ease: The Art of docker-compose

In the previous chapter, we embraced containerization. Now, let's go a step further. It's time to introduce your new best friend for managing multi-container setups: `docker-compose`.

1. Why docker-compose?

- **Complex Setups:** Airflow often involves multiple components:
    - Web Server
    - Scheduler
    - Worker(s)
    - Database (PostgreSQL, etc.)
    - Maybe a message broker (Redis/RabbitMQ)
- **Coordination is Key:** `docker-compose` lets you define and manage the relationships between these containers in a single place.

2. The Magic File: `docker-compose.yml`

- **Language of Orchestration:** Compose files use YAML format to describe your multi-container setup.
- **Key Sections:**
    - `version`: Specifies the `docker-compose` file format.
    - `services`: Here, you define each component as a service.

3. A Sample `docker-compose.yml` for Airflow

```yaml
version: '3'
services:
  postgres:  # Database service
    image: postgres:14
    environment:
      - POSTGRES_USER=airflow
      - POSTGRES_PASSWORD=airflow
      - POSTGRES_DB=airflow
    volumes:
      - ./postgres-data:/var/lib/postgresql/data

  redis: # Example message broker
    image: redis:7

  webserver:
```

```
      image: apache/airflow:2.4.3
      depends_on:
        - postgres
        - redis
      ports:
        - "8080:8080"
      volumes:
        - ./dags:/opt/airflow/dags
      environment:
        - AIRFLOW__CORE__EXECUTOR=CeleryExecutor
        # ... other config ...

  worker:
      image: apache/airflow:2.4.3
      depends_on:
        - redis
      environment:
        - AIRFLOW__CORE__EXECUTOR=CeleryExecutor
        # ... other config ...
```

4. Deciphering the Structure

- **services:** Each component (webserver, worker) is a service.
- **image:** Specifies the Docker image to use.
- **depends_on:** Expresses dependencies (webserver waits for the database).
- **ports:** Maps container ports to your host machine.
- **volumes:** Manages data persistence across containers.
- **environment:** Sets environment variables for each service.

4. Compose in Action

- **Up and Running:** `docker-compose up -d` (starts all services in detached mode)
- **Changes:** Modify your `docker-compose.yml`, then `docker-compose up -d` to reapply them.
- **Taking Things Down:** `docker-compose down`

Benefits of docker-compose

- **Blueprint:** Your entire infrastructure is codified in a single, versionable file.
- **Simplified Management:** Start, stop, and scale your Airflow setup with ease
- **Cross-Environment Consistency:** Development, production – achieve parity

Practical Exercise

1. **Extend the Example:** Add a Flower service (Airflow monitoring UI) to the sample `docker-compose.yml`.
2. **Experiment:** Try scaling the number of workers with `docker-compose up --scale worker=2`

Additional Resources

- **Docker Compose Documentation:** https://docs.docker.com/compose/
- **Best Practices for Airflow with Compose:**
  https://docs.docker.com/compose/samples-for-compose/

Next Up: Let's start diving into the Airflow User Interface, understanding the dashboards and views Airflow offers!

Section 3:
User Interface Deep Dive

Navigating the Dashboard: Exploring DAGs View

Welcome to your Airflow command center! The DAGs View is where you'll monitor your data pipelines, troubleshoot issues, and interact with the beating hearts of your Airflow system – your DAGs.

Key Concepts to Remember

- **DAG:** The blueprint of your Airflow workflow.
- **Task:** The individual units of work within a DAG.
- **DAG Run:** A specific execution instance of a DAG (with a start time and status).

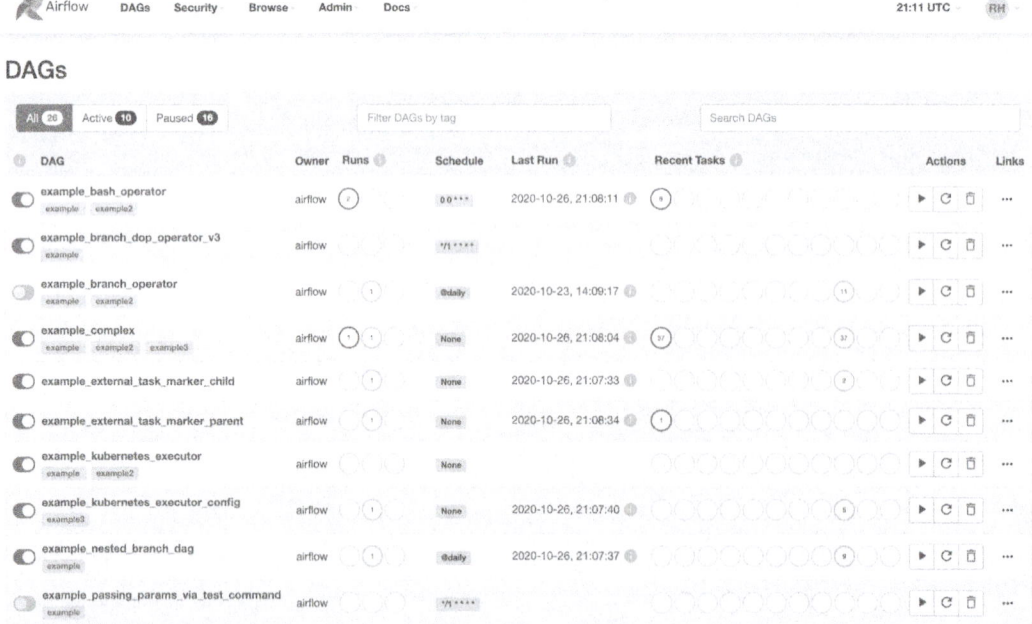

Navigating the DAGs View

1. **DAGs List:**

- Each row represents a single DAG in your AIRFLOW_HOME directory.
- **Status Icons:** Provide quick visual cues (running, success, failed).
- **Quick Actions:** Trigger manual runs, refresh the status, or delete a DAG.
2. **Graph View Button:** Takes you to a visual representation of your DAG (more on this in a later chapter!)
3. **Tree View Button:** Offers a hierarchical task-level view of your DAG.
4. **Search:** Filter your DAGs list to quickly find what you need.
5. **Information Panel (Right Side):**
    - **DAG Details:** Schedule interval, recent runs, basic metadata.
    - **Task Instances:** Clicking on a DAG run here dives deeper, showing its individual tasks and their statuses.

Key Information at Your Fingertips

- **Overall DAG Status:** Is my pipeline running as expected?
- **Recent Runs:** History and patterns of success/failure.
- **Run Duration:** Are things taking longer than expected?
- **Broken down by Task:** Pinpoint bottlenecks or problematic areas.

Actions You Can Take

- **Triggering DAG Runs:** Execute a DAG run on demand, even outside of its regular schedule.
- **Clearing Task States:** Reset failed or stuck task states if needed.
- **Marking Success/Failure:** Manually override task states for testing or re-run scenarios.
- **View Logs:** Access task logs directly from the UI (invaluable for debugging).

Practical Exercise

1. **Observe Your Airflow UI:** If you have example DAGs, how are they represented?
2. **Trigger a DAG:** Manually run a DAG and monitor its progress.
3. **Explore the Logs:** Click on a task and find its logs.

Additional Resources

- **Airflow UI Overview (Docs):**
  https://airflow.apache.org/docs/apache-airflow/stable/ui.html

Coming Up Next! In the next chapter, "Setting Sail: Launching Your Maiden DAG", we'll dive into the process of writing your first Airflow DAG.

Setting Sail: Launching Your Maiden DAG

Consider this your first voyage into the world of Airflow automation. We'll keep things simple to solidify the core concepts.

Prerequisites

- You have a running Airflow installation.
- You understand the basics of Python.

Step 1: A Place for Your DAG

- Remember your AIRFLOW_HOME directory? That's where your DAGs will live.
- Create a Python file within that directory. Let's name it my_first_dag.py

Step 2: The Essential DAG Structure

```python
from datetime import datetime

from airflow import DAG
from airflow.operators.python import PythonOperator

# A function to greet
def greet():
    print("Hello, Airflow!")

# DAG Definition
with DAG(
    dag_id="my_first_airflow_dag",
    start_date=datetime(2023, 4, 13), # Replace with desired start date
    schedule_interval="@daily",
    catchup=False # No catching up on past runs
) as dag:

    # Create the task
    greeting_task = PythonOperator(
        task_id="greet_task",
        python_callable=greet
    )
```

Step 3: Breaking it Down

- **Imports:** Bringing in the necessary Airflow modules.
- **A Simple Function:** This could represent any bit of work your DAG might do.
- **DAG Instantiation:**
    - `dag_id`: A unique identifier.
    - `start_date`: When the DAG should begin scheduling.
    - `schedule_interval`: Our example uses `@daily`.
    - `catchup`: Decides if missed runs should be backfilled.
- **PythonOperator:** A versatile operator to execute Python functions
    - `task_id`: Unique identifier for the task.
    - `python_callable`: The function this task will execute.

Step 4: Find It in the UI

- Airflow periodically scans your `AIRFLOW_HOME`. Your new DAG should appear on the DAGs View!

Step 5: Takeoff!

- **Trigger the Run:** Use the "Trigger DAG" action on the UI.
- **Check the Logs:** Click on the task instance and explore the logs. Did your greeting get printed?

Let's Expand: A Slightly More Useful DAG

```python
from datetime import datetime

from airflow import DAG
from airflow.operators.bash import BashOperator

with DAG(
    dag_id="example_bash_dag",
    start_date=datetime(2023, 4, 13),
    schedule_interval=None, # No regular schedule, on-demand only
    catchup=False
) as dag:

    list_dir_task = BashOperator(
        task_id="list_directory",
        bash_command="ls -l"
    )
```

- **New Operator:** The BashOperator executes commands directly in your shell.

Important Takeaways

- **DAGs as Code:** Airflow leverages Python to define workflows.
- **The Building Blocks:** DAGs, Operators, Tasks, and their relationships are foundational.

Practical Exercise

1. **Modify:** Change the bash_command, trigger the DAG, and observe the results.
2. **Add a Task:** Introduce another Python function and create a second task using the PythonOperator.

Additional Resources

- **Airflow Operators:**
  https://airflow.apache.org/docs/apache-airflow/stable/concepts/operators.html
- **Scheduling in Airflow:**
  https://airflow.apache.org/docs/apache-airflow/stable/scheduler/index.html

Next Up: We'll explore the Grid View in Airflow – a handy tool for visualizing DAG runs over time.

A Bird's Eye View: Understanding the Grid Perspective

The Grid View in Airflow offers a compact and informative visualization of your DAG runs across time. Think of it as your mission control dashboard for monitoring pipeline health.

1. Finding the Grid View

1. **Navigate to Browse** → **Grid View** (within the Airflow UI).
2. **Select Your DAG:** Use the dropdown to pick the DAG you're interested in.

2. Decoding the Grid

- **Rows:** Each row represents a single DAG run, identified by its start time.
- **Columns:** Each column represents a task within your DAG.
- **Color Coding (The Key!)**
    - Green: Success
    - Red: Failed
    - Yellow: Running
    - Gray: No status yet (e.g., queued, scheduled) or upstream task dependencies unmet.

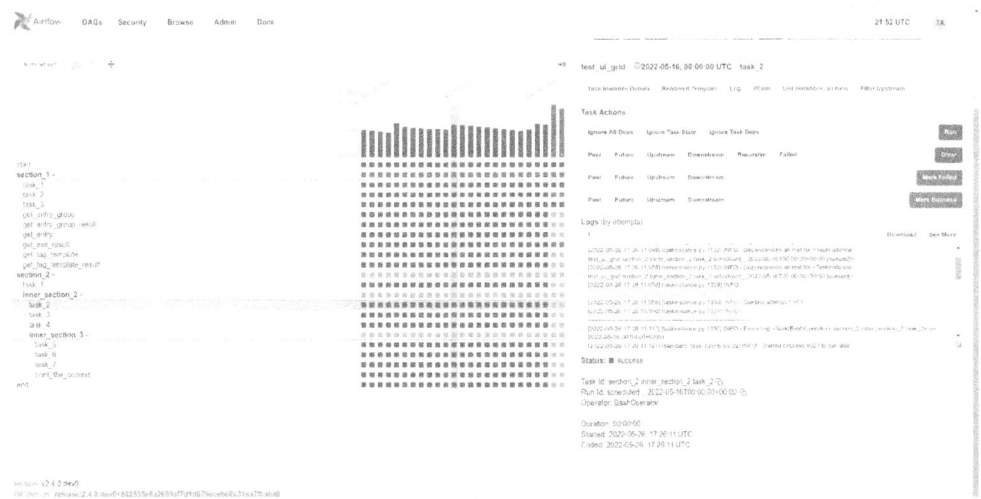

3. Insights at a Glance

- **Overall Health:** Are most runs green? Do failures show a pattern?
- **Task Durations:** Notice tasks that consistently take longer.
- **Recent Activity:** Get a quick snapshot of what ran recently.

- **Bottleneck Spotting:** Observe if certain tasks are often queued or delayed, waiting for others to complete.

4. Grid View in Action

- **Filtering by Date:** Focus on a specific time period.
- **Zooming In:** Click on a grid cell (representing a task instance) to drill down into logs and details for that execution.

When the Grid View Shines

- **Regularly Scheduled DAGs:** The visual patterns become very powerful.
- **Troubleshooting:** Quickly identify when failures started occurring, and which tasks are the culprits.
- **Performance Monitoring:** Spot potential bottlenecks over time.

5. Complementary Views

- **DAGs View:** High-level status of the DAG itself.
- **Graph View:** Understand dependencies and the overall structure of your DAG (more on this soon!)
- **Tree View:** See the status of tasks within a particular DAG run, in a hierarchical view.
- **Gantt Chart:** Visualize task durations for a specific DAG run (more on this later too!)

Practical Exercise

1. **Experiment:** Trigger multiple runs of a DAG and observe how the Grid View updates. Introduce a failure (e.g., make a task raise an exception) and observe the change.

Additional Resources

- **Airflow Documentation: Views**
  https://airflow.apache.org/docs/apache-airflow/stable/ui.html

Up Next: Let's explore the Graph View, where we'll visualize the logical structure and dependencies within your DAG.

Visualizing Relationships: Embracing the Graph View

Sometimes, a textual DAG definition can feel a bit abstract. The Graph View brings clarity, showing how the pieces of your workflow fit together.

1. Accessing the Graph View

- From the DAGs View, click the "Graph View" button next to your desired DAG.

2. Decoding the Visuals

- **Nodes:** Each task within your DAG is represented as a box (node).
- **Arrows:** Arrows indicate dependencies. An upstream task must complete before its downstream task can start.
- **Color Coding:** Provides task status at a glance (similar to the Grid View).

3. The Benefits of a Graphical Perspective

- **Intuitive Understanding:** Even for non-coders, the flow of your DAG becomes clear.
- **Quick Dependency Checks:** See what tasks rely on others and how failures might propagate.
- **Complex DAGs Demystified:** Large workflows are easier to comprehend.
- **Potential Bottleneck Identification:** Visually spot where tasks might pile up due to dependencies.

4. Interactive Features

- **Zooming:** Zoom in and out for big-picture views or detailed inspection.
- **Task Details:** Click on a node to view logs, code snippets, etc.
- **Highlight Dependencies:** Hovering over a task highlights upstream and downstream dependencies.

5. When to Use Graph View

- **Initial Design:** When you're first sketching out a DAG.
- **Debugging:** To understand why a task might be stuck.
- **Explaining Workflows:** Communicating your data pipeline to stakeholders.
- **Refactoring:** To visualize the impact of changes to your DAG structure.

Graph View as a Companion

Think of the Graph View as a visual aid alongside other UI tools:

- **DAGs View:** See the high-level status of your DAG.
- **Grid View:** Monitor patterns of execution over time.
- **Tree View:** Drill into specific DAG runs at a task level

Practical Exercise

1. **Create a DAG with Branching:** Include some branching logic in your DAG (e.g., using the `BranchPythonOperator`). Observe how this is represented in the Graph View.

Additional Resources

- **Graph View in the Airflow UI Docs:**
  https://airflow.apache.org/docs/apache-airflow/stable/ui.html

Coming Up Next! In the next chapter, "Timing is Key: Leveraging Landing Times View", we'll explore a UI feature tailored for a specific data pipeline concept.

Timing is Key: Leveraging Landing Times View

Understanding Landing Times

- **Not Just Execution Time:** In data pipelines, we often care about the time the data itself represents, not just when a task ran.
- **The Concept of a Landing Time:** This is a timestamp associated with a chunk of data produced by your DAG.
- **Example:** A task processing sales from yesterday would have a landing time corresponding to yesterday's date.

Why Landing Times Matter

1. **Data Freshness:** Are you processing data as soon as it's available? Identify delays.
2. **Downstream Dependencies:** Tasks expecting "yesterday's data" can accurately align to this.
3. **Decision Making:** Acting on stale data is dangerous. Landing Times provide clarity.

Finding the Landing Times View

1. **Browse → Landing Times**
2. **Select Your DAG**

Decoding the View

- **Color-Coded Table:** Each cell represents a DAG run, colored based on its data freshness according to thresholds you can configure.
    - Fresh (typically green)
    - Slightly Delayed
    - Severely Delayed
- **Timestamps:** Understand the exact landing time of each execution.

Customizing the View

- **Time Range:** Zoom in on a specific period.
- **Focus:** Choose 'relative' to see delays from the expected landing time, or 'absolute' to see the landing times themselves.

When to Use Landing Times View

- **Daily/Hourly Reports:** Are your reports running with the expected data (`landing_time`)?
- **Time-Sensitive Data:** Spot where processing lags behind the real world.
- **Upstream/Downstream Synchronization:** Ensure dependent DAGs use the correct data versions.

Practical Considerations

- **How Do You Set Landing Times?** This is often done within your task's code using Airflow concepts like `execution_date` and Time Delta calculations. (We'll explore this in later chapters)

Additional Resources

- **Concept of Landing Times (Blog Post):**
  https://www.stitchdata.com/blog/landing-times

Next Up: Let's explore the Calendar View, a visual way to track how DAG runs trigger over the days and months.

Marking the Days: Navigating the Calendar View

Think of the Calendar View as your high-level monthly scheduler, showing exactly when your DAGs have run in an intuitive format.

1. Finding the Calendar View

- Browse → Calendar View

2. Visualizing Your Schedule

- **Color-Coded Days:** Each calendar day is colored based on DAG runs:
    - Green: At least one DAG run succeeded.
    - Red: All DAG runs failed.
    - Gray: No DAG runs were scheduled.
- **Multiple DAGs:** If you select multiple DAGs, the colors will blend to indicate their combined success/failure states.

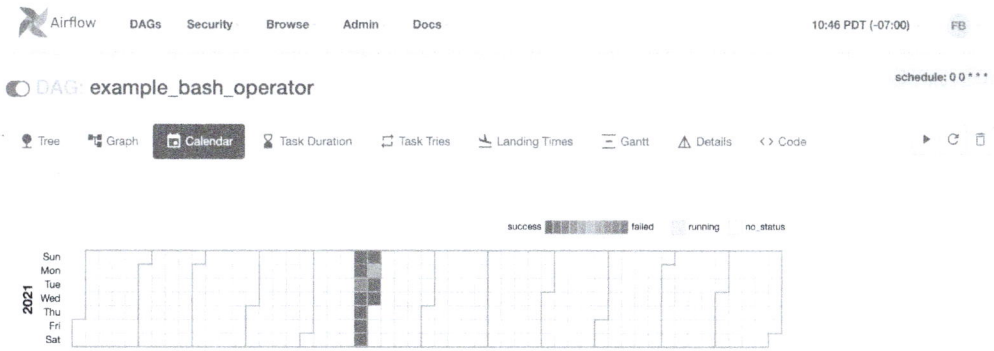

3. When the Calendar View Shines

- **Spotting Unexpected Gaps:** Did a daily DAG miss a day? The calendar highlights this instantly.
- **Identifying Patterns:** Are failures clustered on specific days of the week? This might hint at an external dependency issue.
- **Weekly/Monthly Reporting:** Quickly visually confirm your pipeline ran as expected over a period.

4. Interactive Elements

- **Zooming:** Click on a specific day to see a list of DAG runs for that day with their statuses.
- **Filtering:** Focus on specific DAGs.

5. Complementary Views

It's important to remember that other Airflow views provide different insights:

- **DAGs View:** Overview of your DAGS and recent runs.
- **Grid View:** Status of tasks within specific DAG runs.
- **Graph View:** Logical structure of a DAG

Practical Exercise

1. **Experiment:** If you have a daily DAG, observe how the Calendar View reflects execution over the course of a week.

Additional Resources

- **Airflow Docs on Calendar View:**
  https://airflow.apache.org/docs/apache-airflow/stable/ui.html#calendar-view

In the Next Chapter: Let's explore the Gantt View, where we can visualize the durations of individual tasks within DAG runs.

Time in Motion: Unveiling the Gantt View

Sometimes you need to see how long tasks take within the context of an entire DAG run. The Gantt Chart offers this focused view.

1. Accessing the Gantt View

1. From the DAGs View, find a DAG run of interest (a row in the table).
2. Click the "Gantt View" button.

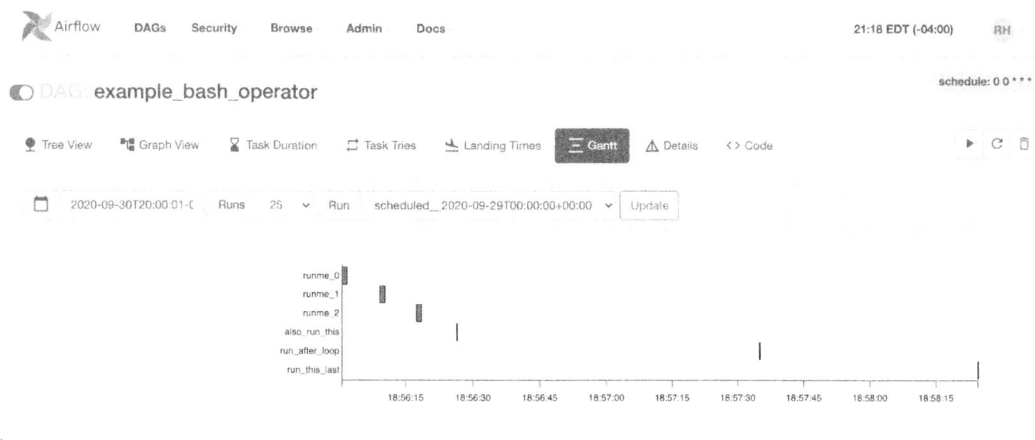

2. Decoding the Gantt Chart

- **Horizontal Axis:** Represents time.
- **Bars:** Each task within the DAG run is shown as a horizontal bar.
    - Length of the bar: Corresponds to the duration of the task.
    - Color: Indicates task state (success, running, failed, etc.).
- **Vertical Ordering:** Tasks are often arranged to loosely match the dependency structure of your DAG.

3. The Power of the Gantt

- **Pinpointing Bottlenecks:** Easily spot tasks that consistently take the longest.
- **Identifying Parallelism (Or Lack Thereof):** See if your tasks execute concurrently as intended.
- **Zooming and Panning:** Change the time range and zoom in for detailed analysis of a specific period during the DAG's execution.

4. When to Use the Gantt View

- **Performance Optimization:** The primary use case for the Gantt View.
- **Understanding Retries:** If a task has retries, the Gantt will display them visually.

- **Debugging Long-Running DAGs:** Identify where things spend the most time.

5. Interactive Features

- **Task Information:** Hover over a bar to see task details, try it out!
- **Log Button:** Click on a bar to jump directly to the logs of that task.

Important Notes

- **Gantt and Grid Are Friends:** Use the Grid View to see patterns across multiple DAG runs, then Gantt to zoom in on a single run of interest.
- **Not Real-Time:** The Gantt chart reflects a past DAG run.

Practical Exercise

1. **Introduce a Delay:** Add a `time.sleep()` statement to a task in your DAG. Observe how this is reflected in the Gantt View.

Additional Resources

- **Airflow Docs: Gantt Chart**
  https://airflow.apache.org/docs/apache-airflow/stable/ui.html

Coming Up Next! In the next chapter "Dive into the Code: Exploring the Code View", we'll examine a way to directly view the Python code that defines your DAG.

Dive into the Code: Exploring the Code View

Airflow DAGs are written in Python. The Code View lets you peek under the hood without even leaving your browser.

1. Finding the Code View

1. **DAGs View:** Click on a DAG of interest.
2. **Click the "Code" button:** This will open a new tab.

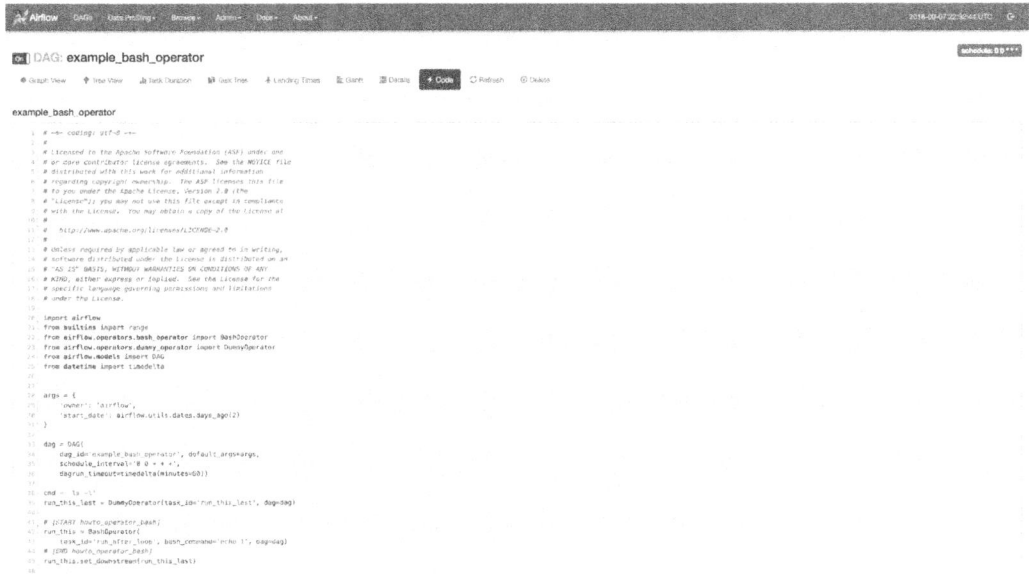

2. What You'll See

- **Formatted Python:** Your DAG code presented in a readable way with syntax highlighting.
- **No Editing:** Think of this as a read-only view for understanding, not editing. (You'll make changes to your DAG files in a code editor.)

3. When the Code View Is Your Friend

- **Understanding a DAG You Didn't Write:** Inherit someone else's Airflow project? The Code View helps you grasp the logic.
- **Debugging:** See the exact code that generates a task. Combine this with logs for troubleshooting.
- **Learning by Example:** The Code View can be a great way to see how others structure their Airflow DAGs.

4. Navigating the Code

- **Line Numbers:** Handy for pinpointing specific sections.
- **Search:** The Code View often has a built-in search function (`Ctrl+F` / `Cmd+F`) to find the operators and tasks you're looking for.
- **Collapsible Sections:** Focus on areas of interest by collapsing code blocks.

5. Code View for Clarity

The Code View complements the other visual tools in Airflow:

- **Graph View:** Overall structure of your workflow.
- **Tree View, Gantt View:** Focus on task execution within runs.
- **Code View:** The raw instructions governing everything.

Practical Exercise

1. **Find an Operator:** Open the Code View for a DAG and locate a specific operator (like `BashOperator` or `PythonOperator`). Can you see its parameters?

Additional Resources

- **Airflow UI Walkthrough (with Code View)**
  https://airflow.apache.org/docs/apache-airflow/stable/ui.html

Next Up: Let's start building a real, working data pipeline! We'll begin by laying the groundwork – understanding DAGs, setting up your environment, and defining the basic workflow.

Section 4:
Crafting Your First Data Pipeline with Airflow

Initiating Your Project: A Prelude to Pipeline Creation

1. **Define Your Data Workflow**

   - **Clarity is Key:** Don't jump into coding just yet. Think about:
     - **The Problem You're Solving:** What business question are you answering, or what process are you improving with this data pipeline?
     - **Inputs & Outputs:** Where does your data come from? Where does it ultimately need to end up? (Databases, files, dashboards, etc.)
     - **Steps Involved:** High-level outline of the transformations, checks, and actions your data will undergo.

2. **Map Out the DAG (Roughly)**

   - **Pen and Paper (or Whiteboard):** Sketch out a basic flowchart of your intended pipeline.
   - **Nodes as Tasks:** Boxes in your sketch will likely become tasks within your Airflow DAG.
   - **Arrows as Dependencies:** Show which tasks rely on the output of others.
   - **Don't Sweat Perfection:** This is just to kickstart your thinking in the structure of an Airflow DAG.

3. **Choose Your Weapons (Technologies)**

   - **Airflow as Orchestrator:** It's the star of the show, but you'll likely need other tools:
     - **Databases:** PostgreSQL, MySQL, etc., for storing data.
     - **Programming Languages:** Python is common within Airflow tasks (but others are possible if needed).
     - **External APIs:** How will you interact with any data sources outside your direct control?

4. Prepare Your Development Environment

- **Local Setup:** Follow the Airflow installation guide from earlier chapters. You'll need a suitable code editor or IDE.
- **Version Control:** Use Git (or a similar system) to track code changes and collaborate if it's a team project.

5. Project Structure

- **Create a Project Directory:** The home for all your DAGs and supporting files.
- **Airflow Home:** Remember your AIRFLOW_HOME environment variable? That's where your DAGs will live.

Example: User Behavior Analysis Project

1. **Problem:** Gain insights into how users interact with a website to improve the user experience.
2. **Workflow**
    - Extract raw website logs.
    - Clean and preprocess the log data.
    - Calculate key metrics (time on site, popular pages, etc.).
    - Store the results in a database.
    - Generate a dashboard visualization
3. **Technologies:**
    - Airflow
    - Python (for data processing)
    - PostgreSQL as a database
    - A dashboarding tool (e.g., Tableau or Superset)

Practical Exercise

1. **Choose a Mini-Project:** Pick a small, well-defined data task (fetching data from a public API, transforming a CSV file, etc.).
2. **Do Steps 1-3:** Define the problem, sketch a DAG, and list required technologies.

Additional Resources

- **Project Organization in Airflow:**
  https://airflow.apache.org/docs/apache-airflow/stable/concepts/projects.html

Setting the Stage: Establishing Your Project Environment

Think of this chapter as preparing your workspace before an intricate construction project begins.

1. The Airflow Home Base

- **Reminder:** Everything Airflow-related (your DAGs, configurations, etc.) lives within the directory specified by your AIRFLOW_HOME environment variable.
- **Creating the Directory (If Needed):**
    - A common location is within your user's home directory (e.g., /home/your-username/airflow)
    - Use a terminal command like: `mkdir ~/airflow`

2. Project Directory

- **Within AIRFLOW_HOME:** Create a dedicated directory for your new data pipeline project.
- **Give It a Clear Name:** Example: `user_analytics_pipeline`

3. Python Environment Preparation

Airflow is heavily Python-based, so let's make sure you're set:

- **Python Installation:** Airflow requires Python (check the Airflow docs for the currently supported versions). If you don't have it, get it installed! (https://www.python.org/downloads/)
- **Virtual Environment (Highly Recommended):**
    - Use `venv` or similar tools to create an isolated environment for your project to avoid conflicts with other Python things happening on your system.

4. Installing Airflow

- **Within Your Environment:** Activate your virtual environment if you're using one.
- **The Magic Command:** `pip install apache-airflow`
- **Providers (As Needed):** If your project will interact with specific databases, cloud services, or other external systems, install the appropriate Airflow providers (e.g., `pip install apache-airflow-providers-amazon`, `pip install apache-airflow-providers-postgres`).

5. Initialize Your Airflow Database

- **From the Command Line:** Navigate to your AIRFLOW_HOME directory.
- **Run:** `airflow db init`. This sets up the database where Airflow keeps track of your DAGs, task statuses, etc.

Example: Setting Things Up on Linux

1. `export AIRFLOW_HOME=~/airflow`
2. `mkdir ~/airflow`
3. `cd ~/airflow`
4. `python3 -m venv pipeline_env`
5. `source pipeline_env/bin/activate` (Activate your virtual environment)
6. `pip install apache-airflow`
7. `airflow db init`

Verification

- **Launch Airflow UI:** Run `airflow webserver` (and optionally `airflow scheduler` in a separate terminal window).
- **Access:** In your web browser, go to http://localhost:8080. You should see the Airflow interface!

Important Notes

- **Detailed Airflow Installation:** See the full installation guide in the Airflow documentation for specifics on your OS.
- **Environment Management:** Get comfortable with creating virtual environments as you'll likely have different projects with potentially different Airflow or dependency requirements.

Additional Resources

- **Airflow Documentation: Setting Up an Environment**
  https://airflow.apache.org/docs/apache-airflow/stable/start/local.html
- **Virtual Environments in Python** https://docs.python.org/3/tutorial/venv.html

Next Up: We'll unveil the DAG – the blueprint of your Airflow workflow!

Unveiling the DAG: Understanding its Significance

What IS a DAG?

- **Directed Acyclic Graph:** A fancy term with simple implications:
  - **Directed:** Tasks within it have defined dependencies (A must happen before B).
  - **Acyclic:** No circular dependencies allowed (you can't have A depend on B, which depends on C, which then depends on A again).
  - **Graph:** A structure made up of nodes (your tasks) and connecting edges (dependencies).

Why Do DAGs Matter?

1. **The Blueprint:** Your entire data pipeline's structure and logic are expressed within a DAG.
2. **Airflow's Language:** Airflow understands DAGs. It knows what to run, when to run it, and what to do if something fails.
3. **Flexibility:** DAGs can model simple linear pipelines, complex branching workflows, and anything in between.

DAGs Are NOT Just Flowcharts

- **Flowcharts are Passive:** They simply illustrate a process visually.
- **DAGs Are Actionable:** Airflow brings your DAG to life by executing the steps it defines.

Key Properties of DAGs

- **ID (dag_id):** A unique identifier for your DAG (must be unique within your Airflow deployment).
- **Tasks:** The individual work units within the DAG, we'll use Operators to define these.
- **Dependencies:** How tasks relate to each other (e.g., Task B must run after Task A).
- **Schedule Interval:** How often the DAG should run (e.g., daily, hourly, etc.)

Example: Data Analysis DAG (Simplified)

```
dag_id = 'user_analysis'
              |
[Task 1: Extract Data]  -->  [Task 2: Clean Data]  --> [Task 3: Generate Report]
```

Airflow Brings DAGs to Life

Think of the DAG as the sheet music, and Airflow as the orchestra:

- **Scheduler:** The conductor, triggering DAG runs per the schedule interval.
- **Executors:** The musicians, actually performing the work of each task.
- **Webserver/UI:** Lets you monitor the concert (see progress, identify wrong notes with retries, etc.).

Practical Exercise

- **Go Back to Your Sketch:** Revisit the workflow sketch you made in the earlier chapter. Can you start identifying the DAG structure within it?

Additional Resources

- **DAGs in the Airflow Docs:**
  https://airflow.apache.org/docs/apache-airflow/stable/concepts/dags.html

In the Next Chapter: Let's construct the basic skeleton of a DAG using Python code!

Framework Foundations: Building the DAG Skeleton

1. Create Your DAG File

- **Naming:** Give it a clear name (e.g., `user_analysis_dag.py`)
- **Location:** Store this file within your project directory, which itself is inside your `AIRFLOW_HOME`.

2. The Essential Imports (Start of your .py file)

```python
from datetime import datetime

from airflow import DAG
from airflow.operators.python import PythonOperator
```

- `datetime`: For working with dates and times (crucial for scheduling!).
- **DAG:** The core Airflow class for defining DAGs.
- `PythonOperator`: A versatile operator for executing Python functions as tasks.

3. Instantiating Your DAG

```python
dag = DAG(
    dag_id='user_analysis',  # Unique ID for this DAG
    start_date=datetime(2023, 4, 18),  # When the DAG should first become active
    schedule_interval='@daily',  # Run every day
    catchup=False  # No backfilling, for this example
)
```

Explanation

- `dag = DAG(...)`: Creates an object named dag, this is your DAG!
- `dag_id`: Must be unique, used by the Airflow UI.
- `start_date`: Indicates when the DAG should first become active and start scheduling.
- `schedule_interval`: Cron expression or one of the presets (@daily, @hourly, etc.) defining how often the DAG runs.

- **catchup:** Controls if Airflow backfills missed runs (more on this later).

4. Dummy Tasks (For Now)

```python
def task_function_1():
    print("This is my first Airflow task!")

def task_function_2():
    print("Look at me, I'm the second task!")

task_1 = PythonOperator(
    task_id='task_1',
    python_callable=task_function_1,
    dag=dag
)

task_2 = PythonOperator(
    task_id='task_2',
    python_callable=task_function_2,
    dag=dag
)
```

- **task_function_1, task_function_2:** Simple placeholder functions. We'll replace these with real work later.
- **PythonOperator:** Creates task objects, ready to be part of your workflow.
    - **task_id:** Unique ID for each task within the DAG.
    - **python_callable:** The function this task should execute.
    - **dag:** Tells the operator it belongs to this DAG.

5. Define Task Dependencies

```python
task_1 >> task_2   # Bit shift operator (>>) sets up "task_1 runs before task_2"
```

What We Haven't Done Yet:

- The task functions don't do anything meaningful.
- We need a way to handle data sources, processing logic, etc.

Practical Exercise

1. **Create the DAG File:** Type out the example code, save it in your `AIRFLOW_HOME`.
2. **Look at the UI:** Does your new DAG (even with silly tasks) show up in Airflow?

Additional Resources

- **Scheduling in Airflow:**
  https://airflow.apache.org/docs/apache-airflow/stable/scheduler/index.html

Next Up: Time to introduce powerful Airflow Operators, the workhorses that will bring your pipeline to life!

Operator Insights: Deciphering their Role

1. What are Airflow Operators?

- **Task Templates:** Operators are blueprints for specific actions within your DAG. They provide a pre-built structure for common data pipeline tasks.
- **Variety:** Airflow comes with a rich set of built-in Operators, and you can even create your own if needed.
- **Not Just Execution:** Operators can also handle things like data transfer, external service interaction, and branching logic.

2. Why Operators Matter

- **Abstraction:** They encapsulate the complexity of carrying out tasks, letting you focus on the bigger picture – the workflow structure.
- **Reusability:** Use the same Operator for similar tasks across multiple DAGs.
- **Community:** Airflow's large community creates and shares Operators (via Providers), saving you development time

3. Common Operator Types

- **BashOperator:** Executes bash commands within your pipeline.
- **PythonOperator:** Runs arbitrary Python functions, giving you maximum flexibility.
- **Sensor Operators:** Wait for conditions to be met before proceeding (e.g., a file to arrive, a database query to return a result).
- **Data Transfer Operators:** Move data between databases, file systems, cloud storage (e.g., `PostgresOperator`, `S3CopyObjectOperator`).
- **External Service Operators:** Interact with APIs, cloud services, and other systems outside of Airflow (e.g., `SlackAPIPostOperator`).

4. Key Operator Properties

- `task_id`: Unique identifier for the task within your DAG.
- `python_callable`: For PythonOperator, this defines the function the task executes.
- `op_args op_kwargs`: Parameters to customize the Operator's behavior (these vary wildly depending on the Operator type).
- `dag`: The DAG the task belongs to.

Let's Enhance Your Example DAG

Imagine a simple part of your workflow is to fetch a CSV file from an external website. Let's modify your DAG to start using Operators:

```python
from airflow.operators.python import PythonOperator
from airflow.providers.http.operators.http import SimpleHttpOperator
# ... (Other imports and basic DAG setup remain the same)

def download_data():
    # Code to download the CSV file

def process_data():
    # Code to load and process the downloaded CSV

download_task = SimpleHttpOperator(
    task_id='download_data',
    http_conn_id='website_download',  # You'll need to configure this connection
    endpoint='data.csv',
    method='GET',
    dag=dag
)

process_task = PythonOperator(
    task_id='process_data',
    python_callable=process_data,
    dag=dag
)

download_task >> process_task  # Set up dependency
```

Important Notes

- **Connections:** Some Operators need pre-configured connections in Airflow to know how to interact with external systems.
- **Providers:** Operators for specific databases, cloud services, etc., are often grouped into Provider packages.

Practical Exercise

- **Airflow Docs Exploration:** Spend some time browsing the Airflow documentation, specifically the available Operators. See if you can find useful ones for your own project.

Additional Resources

- **Airflow Operators Documentation:**
  https://airflow.apache.org/docs/apache-airflow/stable/_api/airflow/operators/index.html

Next Up: We'll explore how to connect Airflow to external data sources and services using Providers and Connections!

Navigating Providers: Choosing the Right Tools

1. What Are Providers?

- **Packaged Expertise:** Provider packages contain collections of Operators, Sensors, and Hooks designed to interact with specific services:
    - Databases: PostgreSQL, MySQL, Microsoft SQL Server
    - Cloud Platforms: Amazon AWS, Google Cloud Platform, Microsoft Azure
    - SaaS Tools: Salesforce, Slack, etc.
- **Community-Driven:** Many providers are maintained by the Airflow community or the service providers themselves, making integration easier.

2. Why Providers Are Key

- **No Reinventing the Wheel:** Providers give you pre-built ways to communicate with common data sources and platforms.
- **Best Practices:** They encapsulate the knowledge of how to interact with these external systems properly.

3. Finding the Provider You Need

- **Airflow Documentation:** The documentation has a comprehensive list of official and community providers. https://airflow.apache.org/docs/stable/
- **Search:** Look for `<service name> airflow provider` (e.g., "BigQuery Airflow Provider").

4. Installing Providers

- **Use pip:** For example, to install the PostgreSQL provider: `pip install apache-airflow-providers-postgres`
- **Restart:** Restart your Airflow Webserver and Scheduler for the changes to take effect.

5. Using Operators from Providers

Let's imagine you need to work with Amazon S3 (cloud storage) in your DAG:

1. **Install:** `pip install apache-airflow-providers-amazon`
2. **Import:**

```
from airflow.providers.amazon.aws.transfers.s3_to_redshift import S3ToRedshiftOperator
```

3. **Instantiate within Your DAG:**

```
transfer_to_redshift = S3ToRedshiftOperator(
    task_id='transfer_to_redshift',
    s3_bucket='my-data-bucket',
    s3_key='data_file.csv',
    redshift_conn_id='my_redshift_connection',
    # ... other parameters
    dag=dag
)
```

Important! Connections

Many Operators from Providers require pre-configured connections within Airflow to know the credentials and addresses of external systems. You manage connections through the Airflow UI.

Example: PostgreSQL Provider

The PostgreSQL provider might give you Operators like:

- **PostgresOperator:** Execute SQL queries on a PostgreSQL database.
- **PostgresHook:** Provides a lower-level interface for interacting with PostgreSQL (useful for custom tasks).

Practical Exercise

1. **Identify Services:** Look back at your project plan. What external services will your data pipeline need to interact with?
2. **Search for Providers:** See if there are Airflow providers available for those services.

Additional Resources

- **List of Airflow Providers:**
  https://airflow.apache.org/docs/apache-airflow-providers/stable/providers/index.html

Next Up: Let's see how to create database tables, essential for many data pipelines, directly from within your Airflow DAGs!

Blueprint for Data: Creating Tables with Precision

1. Why Create Tables from Airflow?

- **Pipeline as Master Plan:** Your DAG becomes the source of truth for your data infrastructure.
- **Versioning:** Changes to your table structure live alongside your DAG code.
- **Automation:** No need to switch tools; create tables as part of the same process that will fill them!

2. Methods

- **Operators from Providers:**
    - Many database providers (e.g., Postgres, MySQL) offer Operators specifically designed for tasks like CREATE TABLE.
    - Example: `PostgresOperator`.
- **General-Purpose Operators:**
    - `BashOperator`: Run command-line tools for your database to execute the necessary SQL commands.
    - `PythonOperator`: Use your database system's Python library (if available) to issue CREATE TABLE statements.

3. The SQL Alchemy Option

- **Airflow + SQL Alchemy:** A powerful combination, especially if you're already using Python for data processing.
- **Define Models:** SQL Alchemy lets you define database tables as Python classes.
- **Migrations:** Consider using a database migration tool (like Alembic) to manage changes to your table schemas over time with Airflow DAGs triggering migrations.

Example: Creating a PostgreSQL Table

Let's use the PostgreSQL provider:

```
from airflow.providers.postgres.operators.postgres import PostgresOperator

create_users_table = PostgresOperator(
    task_id='create_users_table',
    postgres_conn_id='my_postgres_connection',
```

```
    sql = """
        CREATE TABLE IF NOT EXISTS users (
            user_id INTEGER PRIMARY KEY,
            username VARCHAR(50) NOT NULL,
            email VARCHAR(255) UNIQUE
        );
        """
)
```

Important Considerations

- **Idempotency:** Design your table creation tasks so they can be safely run multiple times (e.g., use CREATE TABLE IF NOT EXISTS)
- **Permissions:** Make sure the Airflow user (the one running the tasks) has sufficient privileges in your database to create tables.

Practical Exercise

1. **Design Your Tables:** Sketch out the basic table structures you'll need for your project (columns, data types, basic constraints).
2. **Choose Your Method:** Decide if you want to use provider-specific Operators, general Operators, or consider SQLAlchemy.

Additional Resources

- **SQL Alchemy Tutorial:** https://www.sqlalchemy.org/
- **Database Migrations:** https://alembic.sqlalchemy.org/en/latest/

Next Up: We'll learn how to make Airflow interact with the external sources from where it'll pull in data. We'll do this using Connections!

Establishing Connections: Bridging Data Sources

1. **What Are Airflow Connections?**

   - **Reusable Credentials:** Think of them as saved logins for external systems. They store:
     - Connection Type (e.g., Postgres, AWS, HTTP)
     - Hostname
     - Username
     - Password (encrypted within Airflow)
     - Port
     - Other connection-specific extras
   - **Centralized Management:** You manage connections through the Airflow UI.
   - **Security:** Connections are a safer way to manage sensitive info than hardcoding it into your DAGs.

2. **How Connections Are Used**

   - **By Operators:** Many Operators require a conn_id argument, which references an existing connection.
   - **Behind the Scenes:** When a task runs, Airflow fetches the connection details and supplies them to the Operator.

3. **Creating Connections**

   1. **Airflow UI:** Navigate to the **Admin → Connections** section.
   2. **Click "Add a new record"**
   3. **Fill in the Details:**
      - Conn Id: Unique identifier (this is what you'll use in your DAG code)
      - Conn Type: Choose the appropriate connection type.
      - Provide the host, username, password, etc. for what you're connecting to.

4. **Common Connection Scenarios**

   - **Databases:**
     - Connections IDs like: my_postgres_database, analytics_redshift
   - **Cloud Services:**
     - Connection IDs like: aws_default (using your AWS credentials), gcp_project
   - **REST APIs:**

- Connection IDs like: `public_weather_api`, `company_crm`

Example: Postgres Connection in Your DAG

```
from airflow.providers.postgres.operators.postgres import PostgresOperator

task = PostgresOperator(
    task_id='run_query',
    postgres_conn_id='my_postgres_database',
    sql = "SELECT * FROM important_table;"
)
```

Important Notes

- **Secrets Management:** For extra security, consider integrating Airflow with a secrets management tool like HashiCorp Vault or AWS Secrets Manager.
- **Environment Variables:** Airflow can fetch connection values from environment variables.

Practical Exercise

1. **List Your Data Sources:** Go back to your project sketch and identify all the external systems you'll interact with.
2. **Try Creating Connections:** Experiment creating some practice connections in your Airflow UI, even if placeholder values, to get the hang of it.

Additional Resources

- **Airflow Connections Documentation:**
  https://airflow.apache.org/docs/apache-airflow/stable/concepts/connections.html

Next Up: Let's see how to turn the theoretical creation of tables from the last chapter into reality!

Executing Tasks: Implementing Table Creation

1. Revisiting Your Table Creation Tasks

Let's assume you defined SQL table creation statements within Operators in your previous DAG, such as:

```python
from airflow.providers.postgres.operators.postgres import PostgresOperator

create_users_table = PostgresOperator(
    task_id='create_users_table',
    postgres_conn_id='my_postgres_connection',
    sql = """
        CREATE TABLE IF NOT EXISTS users (
            user_id INTEGER PRIMARY KEY,
            username VARCHAR(50) NOT NULL,
            email VARCHAR(255) UNIQUE
        );
    """
)
```

2. Running Your DAG

There are several ways to trigger the execution of your DAG:

- **Manually from the UI:** Navigate to the DAG in the Airflow web interface, and click the "Play" button.
- **Scheduled:** If your DAG has a schedule interval, Airflow's Scheduler will automatically trigger it at the appropriate times.
- `airflow dags trigger`: Use the Airflow CLI to initiate a DAG run.

3. Behind the Scenes

When your DAG run starts and the `create_users_table` task gets its turn:

1. **Airflow Worker Fetches:** A Worker process grabs the task to execute it.
2. **Connection Established:** Airflow looks up the `my_postgres_connection` connection details.
3. **Database Command:** The `PostgresOperator` sends your `CREATE TABLE ...` SQL statement to your PostgreSQL database.

4. **Database Does Its Thing:** Your database system receives the command and creates the table.

4. Verifying Success

- **Airflow UI:** Check the task status in the Grid View, Tree View, or Graph View. A green success box means all went well.
- **Database Tools:** Use a database client or management tool to directly connect to your PostgreSQL database and check if the `users` table now exists.

Troubleshooting

- **Permissions:** Ensure the database user associated with your Airflow connection has permissions to create tables.
- **Logs:** Airflow provides detailed logs for each task. Check these if anything goes wrong!
- **Testing Connectivity:** Outside of Airflow, try making a simple database connection with the credentials used in your Airflow connection. This isolates Airflow-specific issues from database connectivity problems.

Practical Exercise

1. **Trigger a DAG Run:** Use one of the methods described above to intentionally run your DAG.
2. **Inspect the Logs:** Dig into the task logs in the Airflow UI – get comfortable with understanding what they tell you.
3. **Verify:** Connect to your database and see if your newly created table is there!

Additional Resources

- **Airflow Task Logs:**
  https://airflow.apache.org/docs/apache-airflow/stable/logging-monitoring/logging.html

Next Up: Let's introduce Sensors to make our pipeline more robust by ensuring that data is available before we attempt to process it!

Sensor Sensibility: Detecting Data Availability

1. Why Sensors Matter

- **Data-Driven Pipelines:** Sensors prevent tasks from running prematurely if the data they rely on isn't ready yet.
- **Resilience:** They help your pipeline gracefully handle delays or fluctuations in external data sources.
- **No Wasted Effort:** Sensors prevent tasks from starting only to fail due to missing dependencies – saving you compute resources.

2. How Sensors Work

- **Continuous Poking:** A sensor task repeatedly 'pokes' or checks the state of something at a set interval (e.g., every 30 seconds).
- **The Green Light:** Once the condition the Sensor is monitoring becomes true, the sensor succeeds, allowing downstream tasks to proceed.
- **Timeout (Optional):** You can set timeouts to prevent Sensors from waiting forever.

3. Common Sensor Types

- **ExternalTaskSensor:** Waits for a task in a different DAG or even a different Airflow environment to complete.
- **HttpSensor:** Checks if an HTTP endpoint returns a certain status code or response.
- **S3KeySensor:** Monitors for a specific file (key) to arrive in an Amazon S3 bucket.
- **SqlSensor:** Executes a SQL query, waiting for it to return a certain value
- **TimeSensor:** Waits until a specified time.

4. Sensor in Action: Waiting for an API

Let's say you need to fetch data from an external API before starting your processing.

```python
from airflow.providers.http.sensors.http import HttpSensor

check_api_availability = HttpSensor(
    task_id='check_api_availability',
    http_conn_id='external_api',
    endpoint='/data-ready',
```

```
    response_check=lambda response: response.status_code == 200,  # Success condition
    poke_interval=30,  # Check every 30 seconds
    dag=dag
)
```

5. Integrating Sensors into Your DAG

You place Sensors upstream of the tasks that depend on the resource they're monitoring:

```
check_api_availability >> process_data
```

Important Considerations

- **Timeouts:** Always evaluate if timeouts are necessary for your Sensors to avoid hanging your DAG indefinitely.
- **Custom Sensors:** If existing Sensors don't fit your needs, you can create your own by subclassing `airflow.sensors.base.BaseSensorOperator`.

Practical Exercise

1. **Where Do You Depend?** Examine your pipeline. Are there tasks that absolutely should not run until some external data or file is available?
2. **Find the Right Sensor:** Browse the Airflow documentation for Sensors. See if there are ones that match your dependency needs.

Additional Resources

- **Airflow Sensors Documentation:**
  https://airflow.apache.org/docs/apache-airflow/stable/macros-ref.html

Next Up: Let's make that Sensor even more robust by building a specific check for our hypothetical API!

Assessing Availability: Checking API Access

1. Beyond Just "API is Up"

A basic `HttpSensor` can tell you if a web endpoint responds. But data pipelines often need to be sure the API is ready to deliver the *correct* data.

2. A More Refined Check

Let's enhance your Sensor to be more rigorous. Instead of just a `response_check`, we'll write a custom function:

```python
from airflow.providers.http.sensors.http import HttpSensor

def check_api_content(response):
    import json
    response_json = json.loads(response.content)
    if response_json.get('status') == 'data_ready':
        return True
    else:
        return False

check_api_availability = HttpSensor(
    task_id='check_api_availability',
    http_conn_id='external_api',
    endpoint='/data-ready',
    response_check=check_api_content,  # Our custom check
    poke_interval=30,
    dag=dag
)
```

Explanation

- **check_api_content:** This function now examines the JSON response from the API. It specifically looks for a 'status' field set to 'data_ready'.
- **Failure:** If the API doesn't signal readiness, the function returns `False`, telling the `HttpSensor` to keep waiting.

3. The Importance of Specific Checks

- **Avoid Premature Processing:** This prevents your pipeline from grabbing incomplete or outdated data.
- **Informative:** A well-designed check can tell you if the API is perhaps missing an expected field, or the data is in an incorrect format.

4. Customizing for *Your* API

Adapt the `check_api_content` function to the specific response structure and success indicators of the API you're working with. You may want to check for:

- **Presence of Specific Data Fields:** Ensure required data elements exist.
- **Data Ranges or Values:** Are values within expected bounds?
- **Freshness:** Does the response contain a timestamp that indicates the data is recent?

Important Considerations

- **Error Handling:** What should your pipeline do if the API never signals readiness? Consider adding a timeout to the Sensor.
- **Alerts:** You might want to investigate more sophisticated error alerting mechanisms for when your critical data source is misbehaving.

Practical Exercise

1. **API Contract:** Do you know the promised structure of the API response? List the key elements and how you'd signal success or failure.
2. **Update Your Check:** Modify the `check_api_content` function to match your API.

Up Next: Let's see what it takes to actually pull in that data once the Sensor gives us the all-clear!

Sensing Success: Implementing API Availability Sensor

1. **The Power of the `HttpSensor`**

   - **Purpose:** To ensure that your external API is not only reachable but actively serving the data you expect, prior to triggering downstream processes.
   - **Resilience:** Prevents your pipeline from failing because it tried to grab data that wasn't there yet.

2. **Scenario: Fetching User Data**

Let's imagine your first major task in the pipeline is to pull in a batch of user data from an API. Here's how the `HttpSensor` fits in:

```
from airflow.providers.http.sensors.http import HttpSensor
from airflow.providers.http.operators.http import SimpleHttpOperator
# ... rest of your imports

check_api_availability = HttpSensor(
    task_id='check_api_availability',
    http_conn_id='user_api',
    endpoint='/data-ready',
    response_check=check_api_content, # (From previous chapter)
    poke_interval=30,
    dag=dag
)

fetch_user_data = SimpleHttpOperator(
    task_id='fetch_user_data',
    http_conn_id='user_api',
    endpoint='/user_data',
    method='GET',
    dag=dag
)

check_api_availability >> fetch_user_data  # Dependency established
```

Explanation

1. `check_api_availability`: The Sensor task repeatedly checks for the `/data-ready` endpoint and uses your custom `check_api_content` function to ascertain true readiness.
2. `fetch_user_data`: This task, using the `SimpleHttpOperator`, actually makes the call to get the user data.
3. `>>` : Crucially, we establish a dependency. The data fetch task will only start once the Sensor reports success.

3. Best Practices

- **Specific `response_check`:** Tailor your checks for the structure of your API responses.
- **Meaningful Endpoints:** If possible, work with the team maintaining the external API to design a dedicated endpoint that signals 'data ready' clearly.
- **Timeouts:** Prevent your pipeline from hanging indefinitely if the API becomes unresponsive.

4. Beyond Availability

The `HttpSensor` is a powerful tool, but remember:

- **Data Quality:** Even if data is available, it could be corrupt or incomplete. Consider additional checks after you fetch the data.
- **Complex Data Sources:** For more than simple API calls, you may need custom Operators to interact with external systems reliably.

Practical Exercise

1. **Test Your Understanding:** If the API isn't ready, what would you observe in the Airflow UI as your DAG runs?

Additional Resources

- `SimpleHttpOperator`:
  https://airflow.apache.org/docs/apache-airflow-providers-http/stable/operators/simple_http_operator/index.html

Next Up: Time to actually grab that user data!

Data Extraction Essentials: Retrieving User Data

1. The Heart of Data Pipelines

Data extraction is where the rubber meets the road. It's the process of:

- **Acquiring:** Getting data from its source (APIs, databases, files, etc.).
- **Transferring:** Bringing it into the context of your Airflow workflow for processing.

2. Mastering API Interactions with `SimpleHttpOperator`

Since, in our project, you're fetching user data from an API, let's focus on the `SimpleHttpOperator`:

```python
from airflow.providers.http.operators.http import SimpleHttpOperator

fetch_user_data = SimpleHttpOperator(
    task_id='fetch_user_data',
    http_conn_id='user_api',
    endpoint='/user_data',
    method='GET',
    response_filter=lambda response: json.loads(response.text), # Process the response
    dag=dag
)
```

Explanation

- `http_conn_id`: References the Airflow Connection you configured for the user data API.
- `endpoint`: The specific path within the API you're targeting.
- `method`: 'GET' is common for retrieving data.
- `response_filter`: A simple function to take the raw text response and parse it into JSON.

3. Important Considerations

- **Authentication:** Many APIs require authentication. Airflow Connections let you manage these credentials securely.

- **Pagination:** If the API has large datasets, you might need multiple calls with parameters to fetch everything.
- **Data Formats:** APIs might serve JSON, XML, or other formats. Adjust your parsing accordingly.

4. Beyond `SimpleHttpOperator`

- **Provider Packages:** Often contain Operators tailored to specific databases, cloud services, and SaaS platforms.
- **Custom Python:** For complex extractions, a `PythonOperator` gives you full flexibility (but remember that those Python functions will execute on your Airflow workers!).

5. Tips for Success

- **Understand the API:** Read the documentation for the API you're interacting with.
- **Incremental Testing:** Fetch a small amount of data first to validate your extraction logic works before doing large pulls.
- **Error Handling:** What happens if the API is down? Consider retries or failure notifications.

Practical Exercise

1. **API Exploration:** Dig into the documentation for the API you're using. Note down authentication methods, rate limits, and the exact format of the data it returns.

Additional Resources

- **Airflow Operators Overview:** Explore other operators you might use for data extraction
  https://airflow.apache.org/docs/apache-airflow/stable/concepts/operators.html

User Processing: Transforming Data for Insight

1. Not Just Moving Data, Creating Value

Data processing is where your pipeline shifts from simply handling data to generating the knowledge your business needs. This might involve:

- **Cleaning:** Fixing inconsistencies, handling missing values, etc.
- **Transformations:** Calculating demographics, aggregations (e.g., counts of users by country).
- **Enrichment:** Joining your user data with other data sources to add context.

2. The Likely Tool: PythonOperator

The PythonOperator provides the ultimate flexibility. Let's imagine a processing scenario:

```python
from airflow.operators.python import PythonOperator

def process_user_data(ti):
    import pandas as pd
    user_data = ti.xcom_pull(task_ids='fetch_user_data')  # Get data from previous task
    df = pd.DataFrame(user_data)
    # ... (Do cleaning, calculations, etc.)
    ti.xcom_push(key='processed_data', value=df.to_json())  # Store the result

process_data = PythonOperator(
    task_id='process_user_data',
    python_callable=process_user_data,
    dag=dag
)
```

Explanation

- **XCOM (within the function):** We use this mechanism (explained more in a later chapter!) to grab the data fetched by the earlier task and to pass the processed data downstream.
- **Pandas (just an example):** A common Python library for data manipulation. Your logic might use different libraries.

3. Considerations

- **Library Choices:** Pick the right Python libraries for your analysis type (Pandas, NumPy, Scikit-learn, etc.).
- **Complexity vs. Maintainability:** Complex processing might warrant several tasks for clarity instead of cramming everything into one.
- **Processing Location:** Should processing happen on an Airflow worker, or do you push it out to an external service or a database?

4. Beyond the PythonOperator

- **Database Operators:** If your processing logic is expressible in SQL, Operators for your specific database (e.g., `PostgresOperator`) can be efficient.
- **Spark Integration:** Airflow can interact with Spark clusters for heavy-duty, distributed processing.

5. Test, Test, Test!

Data processing can get complex. It pays off to:

- **Unit Tests:** Test your Python function in isolation with sample inputs and expected outputs.
- **Integration Test:** Run your task on a small data set within the DAG to catch unexpected edge cases.

Practical Exercise

1. **Outline Your Logic:** Think of 3-5 key transformations you want to make on the raw user data. Don't code yet, just write them in plain language.

Additional Resources

- **XCOM in Airflow:** Get a sense of the mechanism for passing data between tasks
  https://airflow.apache.org/docs/apache-airflow/stable/concepts/xcoms.html

Next Up: Let's talk about where to put that valuable processed data and ensure your processing steps happen reliably in the context of your entire pipeline!

Preparing for Execution: Prerequisites for User Processing

1. Dependencies: Not Just Code

Before your processing task can start, ensure:

- **Data Availability:**
    - The Sensor we built earlier should guarantee your user data is fetched.
    - Do you depend on other data sources being ready? Consider adding more Sensors if needed.
- **Environment Setup:**
    - Have you installed the Python libraries (Pandas, etc.) required by your processing logic? Airflow environments help manage this.
    - Are external systems (like a database for temporary results) accessible and configured correctly?

2. Workflow Integration: The Power of the DAG

In your DAG file:

```
check_api_availability >> fetch_user_data >> process_user_data
```

- **Upstream/Downstream:** The >> symbols establish that your processing task depends on the successful completion of data fetching.

3. The Importance of Idempotency

- **What if Things Go Wrong?** Tasks might fail due to temporary glitches. Design your processing to be repeatable. For example:
    - Can you resume processing from where you left off if interrupted?
    - Do you produce the same clean results even if run multiple times on the same input data?

4. Considerations for Scale

- **Data Size**: Does a small test dataset misrepresent the processing time and resource usage when dealing with real-world data volumes?
- **Output:** Where does your processed data go? Is that destination ready to handle the amount you'll send?

5. Tips

- **Version Control:** Use Git (or a similar system) for your DAGs and processing code. This helps rollback if changes cause problems.

- **Small Tests First:** Start by processing a tiny subset of data to ensure your core logic works, *then* worry about scaling up.

Practical Exercise

1. **List Your Dependencies:** Explicitly list any libraries, external systems, or even specific file formats your user processing task requires.

Additional Resources

- **Airflow Task Idempotency:**
  https://airflow.apache.org/docs/apache-airflow/stable/concepts/task-instance.html#task-idempotence

Processing Prowess: Implementing User Processing

1. Revisiting Your `process_user_data` function

Let's assume your Python function looks something like this:

```python
import pandas as pd

def process_user_data(ti):
    user_data = ti.xcom_pull(task_ids='fetch_user_data')
    df = pd.DataFrame(user_data)

    # Data Cleaning
    df.dropna(subset=['email'], inplace=True)  # Example

    # Transformations
    df['registration_country'] = df['address'].apply(lambda x: x.get('country', 'Unknown'))

    # ... more of your processing logic ...

    processed_data = df.to_json(orient='records')
    ti.xcom_push(key='processed_data', value=processed_data)
```

2. The PythonOperator

```python
process_user_data = PythonOperator(
    task_id='process_user_data',
    python_callable=process_user_data,
    dag=dag
)
```

3. Key Points

- **XCOM Usage:** We use XCOM to get the raw data pulled in the previous task and to pass the processed data downstream.
- **In-Worker Processing:** This assumes your processing is relatively lightweight and suitable to run directly on an Airflow worker.

4. Beyond the Basics

- **Database Integration:** For complex transformations, you might use a `PostgresOperator` or similar to directly query and update data within your database.
- **External Systems:** If processing involves a specialized analytics platform, you might need custom Operators or Hooks to interact with that system.
- **Scaling Up:** For huge datasets, look into Spark integration with Airflow or delegating processing to a dedicated cluster designed for that workload.

5. Best Practices

- **Modularity:** Break complex processing into smaller functions for better testing and maintainability.
- **Logging:** Use Airflow's logging facilities (or your own) to record important information and errors from within your processing task.
- **Data Snapshots:** Consider periodically saving intermediate processing results in case things go wrong mid-way.

Practical Exercise

1. **Implement Your Logic:** Translate the processing steps you outlined earlier into actual code within the `process_user_data` function.
2. **Test in Isolation:** Write simple unit tests to check your processing function outside of Airflow.

Additional Resources

- **Airflow Logging:**
  https://airflow.apache.org/docs/apache-airflow/stable/logging-monitoring/logging.html

Hooking into Data: Understanding their Functionality

1. Hooks: Your Pipeline's Connections to the World

- **Reusable Interfaces:** Hooks encapsulate the logic of connecting to and interacting with:
    - Databases (MySQL, Postgres, etc.)
    - Cloud services (AWS S3, Azure Blob Storage, etc.)
    - SaaS platforms (Salesforce, Slack, etc.)
    - Even custom or internal systems

2. Why Hooks Matter

- **Abstraction:** They hide the complexities of authentication, API calls, and error handling behind a consistent interface within your Airflow DAGs.
- **Code Cleanliness:** Your task logic stays focused on what to DO with the data, not the nitty-gritty of how to get it.
- **Community Power:** Airflow's Provider packages often contain pre-built Hooks, saving you development time

3. A Hook in Action

Let's imagine you need to fetch some analytics data stored in a simple PostgreSQL database:

```python
from airflow.providers.postgres.hooks.postgres import PostgresHook

def fetch_analytics_data():
    postgres_hook = PostgresHook(postgres_conn_id='analytics_database')
    results = postgres_hook.get_records("SELECT * FROM daily_report")
    # ... process the results
```

Explanation

- **PostgresHook:** A specialized Hook from the Postgres provider.
- **postgres_conn_id:** References an Airflow Connection you've set up.
- **get_records:** A convenient method provided by the Hook to execute a query.

4. Beyond the Basics

Hooks often have methods to:

- **Run SQL queries/commands**
- **Transfer files**
- **Send messages or notifications**
- **Trigger actions in external systems**

5. Considerations

- **Providers:** Check which Providers are relevant to the systems you use
- **Airflow Connections:** You'll need to configure these to give your Hooks the credentials and access details they need.

Practical Exercise

1. **What Do You Connect To?** List 2-3 external systems your pipeline interacts with (or might in the future).
2. **Find the Hook:** Search the Airflow documentation for Providers that might have Hooks for those systems.

Additional Resources

- **Airflow Hooks Documentation:**
  https://airflow.apache.org/docs/apache-airflow/stable/_api/airflow/hooks/index.html

Next Up: Let's explore strategies for reliably and efficiently storing the results of your data processing!

Data Storage Strategies: Saving User Data

1. Not Just Where, But How

Choosing a data storage destination needs to consider:

- **Data Type:** Is your processed data structured (tables), semi-structured (JSON), or unstructured (like raw text)?
- **Volume:** How much data are you generating?
- **Access Patterns:** Will it be analyzed later, used for real-time dashboards, or to serve an application directly?
- **Long-term Needs:** Archival, strict governance requirements, etc.

2. Common Options in Airflow Workflows

- **Databases:**
    - Postgres, MySQL, etc., are great for structured data.
    - Use Operators like `PostgresOperator` to load data directly.
- **Cloud Object Storage:**
    - S3, Azure Blob Storage, Google Cloud Storage are scalable and cost-effective for large datasets or mixed data types.
    - Airflow has Providers for interacting with these.
- **Data Warehouses:**
    - Redshift, Snowflake are designed for analytics. Consider them if complex querying is your primary goal.
- **NoSQL:**
    - For flexible schemas or very specific access patterns, databases like MongoDB might be suitable (Providers often exist for these).

3. A (Hypothetical) Scenario

Let's say your processed user data is structured and you'll primarily use it for generating reports. A database might be a good fit:

```
from airflow.providers.postgres.operators.postgres import PostgresOperator

store_data_task = PostgresOperator(
    task_id='store_processed_data',
    postgres_conn_id='analytics_database',
    sql='INSERT INTO user_insights SELECT * FROM {{ ti.xcom_pull(task_ids="process_user_data") }}'
)
```

4. Beyond the Basics

- **Temporary Storage:** Sometimes, you might need a temporary staging area before the final storage location.
- **File Formats:** CSV, Parquet, JSON... choose what works best for how the data will ultimately be consumed.
- **Data Quality:** Consider adding basic checks to your storage task to catch errors early

5. Important Considerations

- **Integration**: How will downstream systems access this data?
- **Security & Permissions:** Safeguard sensitive data appropriately.
- **Costs:** Storage, especially in the cloud, can add up. Factor this into your architecture.

Practical Exercise

1. **What Are Your Goals?** How do you envision actually USING the processed user data later on? This will guide your storage decision heavily.

Additional Resources

- **Storage Options on Different Cloud Platforms** (Explore docs for AWS (https://aws.amazon.com/products/storage/), Azure (https://azure.microsoft.com/en-us/services/storage/), etc.)

Storing Success: Implementing User Storage

1. Let's Decide: Database Storage

We'll continue the scenario of storing your processed user insights in a database. Let's assume PostgreSQL.

2. Enter the `PostgresOperator`

```
from airflow.providers.postgres.operators.postgres import PostgresOperator

store_data_task = PostgresOperator(
    task_id='store_processed_data',
    postgres_conn_id='analytics_database',
    sql='''
        INSERT INTO user_insights (country, registration_source, ...)
        SELECT country, registration_source, ...
        FROM {{ ti.xcom_pull(task_ids="process_user_data") }}
    '''
)
```

Explanation

- **postgres_conn_id:** References an Airflow Connection to your database.
- **SQL:** We use XCOMs to pull the JSON data. Your SQL might be more complex if further transformations are needed *before* storage.

3. DAG Integration

Make sure your DAG structure looks like this:

```
check_api_availability >> fetch_user_data >> process_user_data >> store_data_task
```

4. Considerations

- **Table Creation:** A task earlier in your DAG (or a separate setup script) likely creates the `user_insights` table.

- **Idempotency:** Can your `store_data_task` run safely multiple times on the same data? This is important for retries!
- **Upserts:** If data needs updating, instead of just inserting, your SQL would use `ON CONFLICT ...` clauses.

5. Beyond Databases

- **Cloud Storage (S3 Example)** Providers often have operators tailored to these services.
- **API Calls:** Sometimes you might send data to a 3rd-party system. A `PythonOperator` (or a custom one) would handle the API logic.

Practical Exercise

1. **Connection Check:** Do you have an Airflow Connection set up for your database?
2. **Write the SQL:** Draft the full SQL statement you would use, even if it includes some placeholders for now.

Additional Resources

- **Airflow Postgres Operator Documentation:**
  https://airflow.apache.org/docs/apache-airflow-providers-postgres/stable/operators/postgres.html

Next Up: Let's ensure your pipeline flows smoothly and that all steps work together as intended!

Sequencing Matters: Ensuring Workflow Integrity

1. Why Order is Key

Data pipelines are like elaborate recipes:

- **Ingredients (Data):** If you don't fetch data before processing it, things break.
- **Steps:** Mixing ingredients before baking them leads to poor results.
- **Dependencies:** Some tasks *rely* on the outputs of others to function correctly.

2. Airflow's Got Your Back: Implicit and Explicit Ordering

- **Implicit:** Airflow analyzes your DAG code. Since you likely wrote it in a logical sequence, Airflow *usually* infers the correct dependencies.
- **Explicit is Better:** For clarity and to prevent surprises as your pipeline grows, use:
  - `>>` and `<<` : The 'bitshift' operators clearly define upstream and downstream tasks (`task1 >> task2`)

3. Troubleshooting Tips

- **The Graph View:** Your best friend for visualizing dependencies. Are things connected as you expect?
- **Task States:** Watch task colors in the UI as your DAG runs. If things get stuck or run out of order, it's a clue something is wrong.
- **Logs:** Tasks log information. Dig into these when problems arise.

4. Beyond Simple Sequencing

- **Branching:** What if you need to do different things based on conditions? Airflow has branching mechanisms (covered later in the book!).
- **Data Readiness:** Your sensors from earlier chapters are a powerful tool in ensuring tasks run only when their input data is truly available.

5. Best Practices

- **Small, Well-Defined Tasks:** Makes dependencies easier to reason about.
- **Test as You Go:** Run your DAG with small data sets as you're building it to catch ordering issues early.
- **Version Control:** This allows you to roll back if changes accidentally break your pipeline's flow.

Practical Exercise

1. **Map Your Dependencies:** Draw a simple diagram of your current DAG, with arrows between tasks clearly showing what depends on what.

Additional Resources

- **Airflow's Dependency Documentation:**
  https://airflow.apache.org/docs/apache-airflow/stable/concepts.html#dependencies

Next Up: Let's see your pipeline in action and understand how Airflow makes it tick over time!

Dynamic DAG Dynamics: Witnessing Your DAG in Motion

1. Not Just a Static Blueprint

Your DAG definition is code, which means:

- **Data Driven:** Task states, successes, failures, and retries are all part of the real-time execution.
- **Time Dependent:** How it runs today might differ from tomorrow if your data or schedule changes.

2. Airflow UI: Your Monitoring Hub

- **Tree View and Graph View:** Visualizations change as your DAG run progresses. Green means success!
- **Gantt Chart:** See the timing and duration of tasks, helping you spot bottlenecks.
- **Task Logs:** Drill down to see exactly what happened in each task.
- **Clearing Tasks:** Resets task states, useful for testing.
- **Triggering DAG Runs:** Kickstart your pipeline on demand.

3. The DAG Run Lifecycle

- **Scheduling:** Airflow's Scheduler regularly checks if any of your DAGs are due to run based on their schedule intervals.
- **Worker Action:** Available Workers pick up tasks and start executing them.
- **State Updates:** As tasks begin, complete, or fail, the DAG run's state is continuously reflected in the UI.

4. Things Don't Always Go to Plan

- **Retries:** Airflow has built-in retry mechanisms if you configure them. Watch how these show up in the UI.
- **Dependencies:** A failed upstream task can block others.
- **Timeouts:** Long-running tasks might get cut off.

5. Mastering DAG Runs

- **Code Changes:** Your DAG is **not** set in stone. Updates will take effect on subsequent runs.
- **Backfilling** (covered later): Lets you re-run over past periods.
- **SLAs:** (Service Level Agreements) Airflow can alert you if DAGs take too long, etc.

Practical Exercise

1. **Trigger a Run:** Manually run your DAG from the Airflow UI.
2. **Observe:** Keep an eye on the Tree or Graph View as it progresses. Can you spot each task transitioning through states?

Additional Resources

- **Airflow Documentation on DAG Runs:**
  https://airflow.apache.org/docs/apache-airflow/stable/concepts.html#dag-runs

Next Up: Let's add some flexibility to *when* your pipeline runs, mastering Airflow's scheduling capabilities!

Scheduling Savvy: Mastering DAG Timing

1. Not Just 'When', But 'How Often'

Airflow DAGs are driven by schedules:

- **Fixed Intervals:**
- "Every day at midnight"
- "Hourly"
- "The 1st of each month"
- **Cron Expressions:** More fine-grained control if needed (but can be less intuitive for beginners)
- **None:** For manual triggering or external events

2. The `schedule_interval`

In your DAG file, you'll likely have something like this:

```
dag = DAG(
    dag_id='my_user_processing_pipeline',
    default_args=default_args,  # Your default arguments if any
    schedule_interval='0 0 * * *'  # Every day at midnight
)
```

3. Time Zones Matter!

- Airflow, by default, runs in UTC. Be mindful of this if your data or users are tied to a specific time zone.
- There are ways to configure time zone aware scheduling in Airflow.

3. Considerations for Your Pipeline

- **Data Availability:** Does your API update on a certain schedule? Align with that.
- **Downstream Systems:** Do they expect data at specific times?
- **Resource Usage:** Schedule heavy workloads during off-peak times if possible.
- **Business Logic:** Align with reporting cycles, etc.

4. Beyond Simple Schedules

- **Sensors:** Can *defer* your pipeline until data is truly ready, even if it's not on a predictable interval.
- `catchup`: Control whether a DAG tries to "backfill" past runs if it was down.
- **Start Dates & End Dates:** For pipelines that should run only for a certain period.

5. Tips

- **Start Simple:** Get your pipeline working on a basic schedule first.
- **Iterate:** Adjust the timing as you understand your system better.
- **Use Airflow Variables:** Can make schedules more configurable.

Practical Exercise

1. **What's Your Ideal Schedule?** Not just the technical side but *why* would you want your pipeline to run at specific intervals?

Additional Resources

- **Airflow Scheduling Documentation:**
  https://airflow.apache.org/docs/apache-airflow/stable/scheduler/index.html
- **Cron Expression Generator:**
  https://www.freeformatter.com/cron-expression-generator-quartz.html

Next Up: What if you need to run the pipeline with historical data? Let's learn about Backfilling!

Filling the Gaps: Navigating Backfilling Techniques

1. Scenarios Where Backfilling Matters

- **New Pipeline:** You've just set up your awesome data processing, but there's existing data to be crunched.
- **Code Changes:** Significant changes to your logic might mean you want to re-process old data.
- **Downtime Recovery:** If your pipeline was offline for a while, it might have missed several scheduled runs.

2. Airflow's Backfilling Tool

Airflow lets you rerun DAGs over a specified date range. It will essentially "pretend" like it's running in the past. Caveats:

- **Data Availability:** Do you *have* the input data for those past dates?
- **Resource Usage:** Backfilling can be a lot of work for your system!

3. How to Backfill

You can trigger backfills from the UI:

- **DAG Runs Tab:** Select a past date and hit "Create"
- **CLI:** Using the `airflow dags backfill` command is more flexible.

4. Considerations

- `catchup`: Control this on your DAG definition. If `False` (often a good default), Airflow won't automatically try to backfill when it starts up.
- **Dependencies:** A task's success in the past might determine behavior in the present. Think this through!
- **External Systems:** Ensure anything your pipeline interacts with can handle being hit with potentially old data.

5. When *Not* to Backfill

Sometimes it's simply not worth it, or even harmful:

- **Massive Datasets:** If it would take weeks to reprocess... is the result valuable?
- **Complex Side Effects:** If downstream systems were significantly changed historically, your old outputs may cause havoc.

Practical Exercise

1. **Is Backfilling Right For You?** Are there any scenarios currently or in the future where you think you'd realistically need to backfill your user processing pipeline?

Additional Resources

- **Backfilling in the Airflow Documentation:** https://airflow.apache.org/docs/apache-airflow/stable/scheduler/backfill/index.html

Next Up: Let's explore how to evolve your pipeline and keep pace with the ever-changing world of data!

Section 5:
Revolutionizing DAG Scheduling

Embracing Evolution: Understanding the Need for Innovation

1. **Change is the Only Constant**

Data-driven businesses are dynamic. Your pipeline will likely face:

- **New Data Sources:** Maybe the API you rely on evolves, or you add additional sources for a richer picture.
- **Shifting Business Logic:** How you calculate those valuable insights might change due to new requirements.
- **Scaling Up:** As data volumes grow, your processing may need optimization.
- **External System Updates:** Databases, tools you connect to… they don't always notify you before making breaking changes!

2. **Stagnation = Fragility**

If your pipeline doesn't adapt:

- **Results Become Incorrect:** Bad data in, bad insights out.
- **Breakdowns:** Changes in the world around it can cause unexpected task failures.
- **Missed Opportunities:** New data or more efficient techniques become impossible to use without modifications.

3. **Strategies for Adaptable Pipelines**

- **Version Control:** Treat your DAG code like any other codebase. Can you roll back if needed?
- **Modularity:** Well-defined tasks are easier to change, extend, or remove.
- **Configuration, Not Hardcoding:** Use Airflow Variables and Connections to make things more flexible.
- **Testing!** Catch issues early as you modify your DAG.

4. **Evolving Responsibly**

- **Gradual Changes:** Where possible, avoid massive rewrites, as they introduce more risk.
- **Downstream Impacts:** Are systems that consume your pipeline's output ready for changes? Communication is key.
- **Monitoring:** Airflow's UI and alerts help you keep an eye on how your system reacts to your updates.

5. Innovation Mindset

- **Stay Curious:** Are there better ways to acquire data? New libraries for processing?
- **Regular Reviews:** Can parts of your pipeline be simplified or made more efficient? Don't optimize prematurely, but don't let it get stale either.

Practical Exercise

1. **What Could Change?** Brainstorm at least 3 things that might realistically change over the next year and would require modifications to your user processing pipeline.

Additional Resources

- **The Importance of Data Pipeline Maintenance** (General concept, not Airflow-specific): https://www.xplenty.com/blog/data-pipeline-maintenance/

Data Dynamics: Unveiling the Significance of Datasets

1. Beyond Just DAGs: Data as a First-Class Citizen

While DAGs define your process, datasets represent the units of data those processes create, consume, and update. Think of them like checkpoints in your pipeline.

2. Why Datasets Matter

- **Explicit Dependencies:** No more guessing if upstream data is ready. A dataset makes it crystal clear.
- **Coordination:** Separate DAGs can synchronize around the production and consumption of datasets.
- **UI Enhancements:** Airflow's new Datasets view (if you're on a modern Airflow version) offers a fresh perspective on how your data pipeline operates.
- **Breaking Down Silos:** Teams can become producers and consumers of data, not just owners of isolated pipelines.

3. A Simple (Hypothetical) Scenario

Imagine your user data processing results in a dataset called `processed_user_insights`. You have another DAG that generates reports based on this. You would:

- **Producer DAG:** Task(s) within this DAG *output* the `processed_user_insights` dataset
- **Consumer DAG:** Task(s) within this DAG would *consume* the dataset, guaranteeing they only run if it's available.

4. Key Concepts

- **URI:** A unique identifier for the dataset, like `s3://my-bucket/reports/2023-11-23/processed_user_insights`
- **Schedule Interval:** You can optionally control how frequently a dataset should be updated.
- **Producers and Consumers:** Becomes very clear in Airflow's UI or when writing your DAG code

5. Considerations

- **Versioning:** How do you handle updates to datasets over time? URIs can play a role.

- **Granularity:** What constitutes a dataset? A single file? A whole table? Choose what makes sense for your use case
- **Not a Storage Solution:** Datasets are about the *metadata* of the data, not the data itself.

Practical Exercise

1. **Map Your Datasets:** Can you break down your current or planned pipeline into potential datasets? Don't worry about perfect URIs yet, just the high-level concepts of what data flows between stages.

Additional Resources

- **Introducing Airflow Datasets:**
  https://airflow.apache.org/docs/apache-airflow/stable/dag-run.html

Next Up: Let's see how we can rethink rigid schedules and make our pipelines data-driven for better efficiency!

Farewell to Routine: Rethinking Schedule Intervals

1. The Limitations of Fixed Schedules

While classic schedules (@daily, etc.) are a start, they can be inefficient:

- **Stale Data:** Your pipeline runs at midnight, but the upstream data gets updated mid-morning. You're making decisions on old information.
- **Unnecessary Runs:** Maybe data is NOT updated daily. You waste resources.

2. Data-Driven to the Rescue

Airflow gives you tools to be more dynamic:

- **Sensors:** Your best friend! Defer tasks until the data they need is truly present.
- **Datasets:** If you're using them, consumer DAGs can react the *moment* a dataset is produced
- **External Triggers:** Airflow's API or other systems can kick off DAGs if needed, instead of waiting for the clock.
- **ExternalTaskSensor:** Sense the completion of tasks in completely separate DAGs for advanced coordination

3. Strategies for Smarter Scheduling

- **Analyze Your Data's Rhythm:** How often does it *actually* change? Align with that if possible, rather than arbitrary intervals.
- **Start Broad, Then Refine:** Maybe begin with a daily run, and introduce sensors once you see the patterns.
- **"Just in Time" Processing:** If speed is critical, aim to process data as soon after it's available as possible.

4. Considerations

- **Downstream Effects:** If reports rely on your DAG, can they cope with irregular timing?
- **Resource Usage:** Frequent runs might be okay off-peak, but not during busy hours
- **Hybrid Approaches:** Perhaps a fixed schedule as a fallback, but sensors or datasets to optimize when possible.

5. Embracing the Shift

Moving to data-driven scheduling means:

- **Adaptability:** Your pipeline reacts to the world, not just the clock.
- **Efficiency:** You avoid processing when there's nothing new to do.

Practical Exercise

1. **Where Could You Be Smarter?** Are there tasks in your pipeline that might run unnecessarily because their input doesn't update as frequently as the schedule?

Additional Resources

- **Airflow's Guide to Scheduling:**
  https://airflow.apache.org/docs/apache-airflow/stable/scheduler/index.html
- **Scheduling Best Practices:** (General, not Airflow-specific, but good concepts):
  https://airflow.apache.org/docs/apache-airflow/stable/best-practices.html#scheduling

Next Up: Let's see how to split your pipeline into data producers and data consumers for scalability and flexibility!

Crafting the Producer DAG: Empowering Data Generation

1. The Source of the Flow

Producer DAGs are the foundation of data-driven pipelines. They are responsible for:

- **Extraction:** Pulling in data from external systems (APIs, databases, file uploads, etc.)
- **Generation:** Creating datasets (simulations, reports, etc.)
- **Transformation:** Sometimes the initial format of the data needs adjustment before it's truly usable downstream.
- **Outputting Datasets:** (If you're using the Datasets feature) Making the results formally available.

2. Design Considerations

- **Data Freshness:** How often does the source data get updated? Align your producer's schedule (or use sensors) to match.
- **Reliability:** If the producer DAG fails, it can starve your whole pipeline. Build in error handling and retries.
- **Bottlenecks:** Is the data generation process itself resource-intensive? You might need a powerful worker or dedicated Celery queue for this DAG.
- **Clarity:** Cleanly separate the 'producing' logic from anything that should only happen *after* the data is ready.

3. Producer DAG in Action (Hypothetical)

Let's say your user data comes from an API. Your producer DAG might have tasks to:

1. **Call the User API:** Using the appropriate Operator (`SimpleHttpOperator` perhaps)
2. **Preprocess the Result:** Clean up the JSON, handle any inconsistencies
3. **Output as Dataset:**
   `s3://my-bucket/user-data/2023-11-23/fresh_data.json`

4. The Power of Separation

By splitting producers and consumers:

- **Updates:** Changes to how you generate data don't break the reports relying on it.

- **Scaling:** Maybe your producer needs to run more often than the heavy-duty processing DAGs.
- **Ownership:** Different teams might be best suited to manage different parts of the pipeline

5. Tips

- **Start Simple, Iterate:** Get the core data flowing, then add sophistication.
- **Don't Neglect Testing:** Ensure the data you produce is in the expected format and quality.

Practical Exercise

1. **What Are Your Producers?** Whether you have them explicitly or not, what are the distinct steps in your pipeline that bring in fresh data from the outside world?

Additional Resources

- **Designing Data Pipelines (General Concepts):**
  https://docs.aws.amazon.com/datapipeline/latest/DeveloperGuide/what-is-datapipeline.html

Next Up: Let's explore the other side of the coin – DAGs built to consume datasets and do something amazing with them!

Crafting the Consumer DAG: Driving Data Consumption

1. Reacting, Not Just Acting

Consumer DAGs are the workhorses downstream of your data generation. Key characteristics:

- **Input Datasets:** Tasks explicitly consume one or more datasets.
- **Triggered by Updates:** Their schedules (if any) are driven by their dataset's update frequency, or they might use sensors to defer runs entirely until the input is ready.
- **Focus on Transformation:** They do the heavy lifting– analysis, reporting, machine learning, etc.

2. Example: Building on the User Data

Let's continue the scenario where your producer DAG provides a dataset of fresh user data. Your consumer DAG might have tasks to:

1. **Load the User Data:** Read from the dataset's URI.
2. **Calculate Key Metrics:** Lifetime value, engagement trends… whatever is valuable to your business.
3. **Generate Report:** Populate a dashboard or send out a summary email.

3. The Power of Decoupling

Producers and consumers working together give you:

- **Resilience:** Your processing isn't halted entirely if the upstream data has a temporary glitch.
- **Flexibility:** You can add new consumers to an existing dataset without modifying the producer.
- **Clarity:** The pipeline's stages become distinctly visible.

4. Strategies for Consumption

- `ExternalTaskSensor`: Sense when a dataset in another DAG is updated.
- **Schedule-Based, with Cautions:** If a dataset updates frequently, you *can* have the consumer on a schedule, but avoid unnecessary runs if possible.
- **Direct Task Action:** More advanced, but you can write custom Operators that fetch the dataset's payload at runtime.

5. Considerations

- **Error Handling:** What if the dataset is corrupt or incomplete? Your consumer needs to cope gracefully.
- **Versioning:** How do downstream systems know if a report is based on dataset version X or Y?
- **Potential for Stale Data:** If the upstream producer is down for an extended period

Practical Exercise

1. **What to Consume?** Are there datasets implicit in how your pipeline currently works that could be made explicit for greater flexibility?

Additional Resources

- **Airflow Datasets Documentation:**
  https://airflow.apache.org/docs/apache-airflow/stable/index.html

Next Up: Let's see how the Datasets UI gives you a new way to track the health of your data pipelines!

Tracking Tranquility: Leveraging the New View for Dataset Management

1. Beyond Just DAGs

While the classic Airflow UI focuses on the *process* (DAG runs), the Datasets UI brings the *data* itself to the forefront:

- **Which datasets have been updated recently?**
- **Are any producers stalled, preventing downstream work?**
- **See the lineage of how datasets flow through your system**

2. Where to Find It

- Look for a "Datasets" tab in your Airflow UI.
- **Caveat:** If you don't see it, you might be on an older Airflow version that doesn't have this feature.

3. Key Features of the Datasets UI

- **Grid View:** A table-like view showing all your datasets, last update times, schedule, and consumer DAGs.
- **Graph View:** A visual representation of how datasets are connected. Great for spotting bottlenecks or unexpected dependencies.
- **Dataset Details:** Drill down to see specific URIs of past versions, if applicable.

4. Using the View to Troubleshoot

- **Stalled Updates:** A dataset that should update daily, but hasn't? Time to investigate the producer DAG.
- **Orphaned Datasets:** A dataset being produced but nothing consumes it? Maybe it's no longer needed.
- **Unexpected Gaps:** Did a dataset update, but it's missing a chunk of data? This can alert you to upstream source problems.

5. Enhancing Your Dataset Strategy

The Datasets view encourages you to think carefully about:

- **Naming:** Meaningful URIs (including dates or versioning) make things much easier to track.
- **Granularity:** What constitutes a single dataset in your system?

- **Documentation:** While Airflow doesn't *enforce* it, having a clear understanding of what each dataset represents is crucial, especially in larger teams.

Practical Exercise

1. **Map Your Implicit Datasets:** If you're not explicitly using the Datasets feature yet, try sketching out the major data flows in your pipeline. What would the key datasets *be* if you made them formal?

Next Up: What do you do when you need to wait for *multiple* datasets to become available before continuing? Let's investigate!

Patience is a Virtue: Navigating Multi-Dataset Wait Strategies

1. When One Dataset Isn't Enough

There are times when you might need to:

- **Join/Combine:** Data from multiple sources needs to be brought together for analysis.
- **Comparison:** You need the latest snapshot from two different systems to spot discrepancies.
- **Aggregation Over Time:** Perhaps you only generate a report when you have a week's worth of several datasets collected.

2. Strategies

- **Naive Approach (and its dangers):** Have multiple `ExternalTaskSensor` tasks in a DAG, each poking a dataset. This *can* work, but risks tasks getting stuck if one dataset is delayed but others aren't.
- **Branching Logic:** Use a `BranchPythonOperator` or similar to check the states of multiple datasets, and proceed only if everything is available.
- **`TriggerRule` to the Rescue:** Rules like `all_success`, `one_success`, etc. let sensors trigger downstream tasks only when the datasets are in the right state.
- **Dataset Schedule Alignment:** If possible, get upstream producers onto similar schedules to minimize the waiting game.

3. Example: Analyzing User Behavior Across Platforms

Scenario: You get user data from your web analytics AND your mobile app. You need BOTH up-to-date before generating insights.

You could have:

- **Producer DAG 1:** Provides `web_user_data` dataset
- **Producer DAG 2:** Provides `mobile_user_data` dataset
- **Consumer DAG:**
    - Two `ExternalTaskSensor` tasks, one for each upstream dataset.
    - The sensors use the `TriggerRule.ALL_SUCCESS`
    - Downstream tasks then process the combined data.

4. Considerations

- **Timeouts:** Don't let your sensors wait forever. Implement timeouts so stalled datasets don't bring everything to a halt.
- **Alerts:** Have your pipeline notify you if datasets get significantly delayed, impacting downstream reports or processes.
- **Clarity:** Overly complex wait strategies can make your DAGs hard to understand. Look for ways to simplify if possible.

5. Trade-offs

Waiting for multiple datasets can improve data quality but might make your pipeline less responsive to changes in any one particular input. Choose the approach that balances correctness with your business needs.

Practical Exercise

1. **Are You Unnecessarily Waiting?** Are there places in your pipeline where tasks could run as soon as *any* of several inputs are ready, rather than needing all of them?

Additional Resources

- **Airflow Trigger Rules Documentation:**
  https://airflow.apache.org/docs/apache-airflow/stable/concepts.html#trigger-rules

Section 6:
Database Dynamics and Execution Excellence

Executor Essentials: Deciphering their Role in Execution

1. Not Just *What*, but *How*

So far, you've focused on designing your data pipeline's logic. Executors are the powerful engines that determine how the tasks within your DAGs actually get executed. They are fundamentally responsible for:

- **Resource Management:** Do tasks run on the same machine as your Airflow core components, or are they distributed across a separate pool of workers?
- **Concurrency:** How many tasks can execute simultaneously? This is crucial for pipeline efficiency.
- **Scalability:** As the volume or complexity of your data grows, can you easily add more processing power without completely rearchitecting your pipeline?

2. Key Executor Types

Let's reiterate the most common executors and when they are likely the right fit:

- **SequentialExecutor:**
  - The simplest of the bunch. Tasks run one after the other, directly on the machine where your Airflow Scheduler lives.
  - Excellent for initial development and testing, but should never be used for production workloads.
- **LocalExecutor:**
  - Capable of launching tasks as separate processes, providing a degree of parallelism on a single machine. Good for small to moderate-sized pipelines where you don't want the complexity of distributed workers.
- **CeleryExecutor:**
  - The preferred choice for scaling and serious production environments. Uses Celery's distributed task queue architecture, allowing you to have

dedicated worker nodes (even on separate machines) that execute tasks.
- **KubernetesExecutor:**
  - Spins up each task as a self-contained pod within a Kubernetes cluster. Offers tremendous flexibility and dynamic scaling, but be aware it requires managing Kubernetes itself, adding another layer to your infrastructure.

3. Choosing Wisely: Factors to Consider

- **Scale of Your Pipeline:** If you anticipate consistently running a large number of tasks, or if those tasks are resource-intensive, the SequentialExecutor and likely even the LocalExecutor will quickly become bottlenecks.
- **Resource Isolation:** Do some of your tasks have conflicting dependencies or require specialized hardware? Executors like Celery or Kubernetes allow you to isolate tasks for stability.
- **Team's Expertise:** Managing a Kubernetes cluster introduces significant complexity. If your team is not already familiar with it, factor in the learning curve.
- **Flexibility:** Celery lets you have different types of workers (queues) for different types of tasks, giving you fine-grained control over how resources are allocated in larger deployments.

4. The Power of Hybrid Setups

One of the strengths of Airflow is that you don't have to pick a single executor for your entire deployment. This allows you to:

- Use a less complex executor (like LocalExecutor) for lightweight development DAGs or tasks that don't have demanding performance requirements.
- Reserve the power of Celery or Kubernetes for your critical production DAGs, ensuring they have the resources and distribution necessary to run smoothly.

5. Configuration: Where the Magic Happens

Airflow's configuration file holds the keys to controlling executor behavior. Key settings include:

- `core.executor`: Sets your default executor across the installation.
- **Pool Settings:** Allow you to place limits and constraints on resource usage, ensuring tasks don't consume everything and starve each other.
- **Celery Broker/Backend:** Celery needs these to coordinate task distribution between workers and store the results of completed tasks.

Practical Exercise

1. **What's Your Current Executor?** Take a peek at your Airflow configuration file. Can you identify which executor you're using?
2. **Think Ahead:** Even if your current pipeline is small, are there scenarios where you might need the power of a Celery or Kubernetes setup in the future?

Additional Resources

- **Airflow's Executor Documentation:**
  https://airflow.apache.org/docs/apache-airflow/stable/executor/index.html
- **Choosing an Executor (General concepts):**
  https://airflow.apache.org/docs/apache-airflow/stable/concepts.html#trigger-rules

Next Up: Let's unveil some of the secrets within Airflow's configuration files to customize its behavior!

Configuration Chronicles: Unveiling Default Settings

1. The Anatomy of airflow.cfg

- **Your Customization Command Center:** The `airflow.cfg` file is where the majority of Airflow's settings live.
- **Structure:** A mix of sections (e.g., `[core]`, `[webserver]`) and key-value pairs within those sections.
- **Location:** Varies slightly based on your install method. Airflow looks in a few common places for it.

2. Key Sections and What They Control

- **[core]**
    - `executor`: Your default executor across the installation
    - `dags_folder`: Where Airflow looks for your DAG files
    - `sql_alchemy_conn`: Database connection string for Airflow's metadata database.
    - Many other options for plugins, logging, and more!
- **[webserver]**
    - Settings related to how the web interface looks and behaves (authentication, number of items per page in the UI, etc.)
- **[scheduler]`**
    - Fine-tuning of how the Airflow Scheduler itself ticks (heartbeat intervals, DAG parsing frequency)
- ****[celery]`** (If you're using the CeleryExecutor)
    - `celeryd_concurrency`: How many tasks a single worker can run at once
    - `broker_url`: Connection URL for your Celery broker (e.g., Redis, RabbitMQ)

3. Defaults vs. Overriding

- **Sensible Starting Point:** The defaults in `airflow.cfg` try to be reasonable for simple setups, but rarely are they ideal for all production scenarios.
- **Ways to Override:**
    1. **Directly in the file:** Edit the `airflow.cfg` itself.
    2. **Environment Variables:** Certain settings can be overridden with environment variables (prefixed with `AIRFLOW__`)

3. **DAG Level:** Some parameters (`concurrency`, `max_active_tasks_per_dag`, etc.) let you set limits on a per-DAG basis.

4. Common Settings to Be Aware Of

- `dagbag_import_timeout`: Can help prevent deadlocks if your DAGs have complex imports.
- `max_active_runs_per_dag`: Prevents a buggy DAG from flooding your system.
- `default_timezone`: If you're dealing with time-sensitive data, make sure this matches your expectations.
- `parallelism`: Sets a global limit on task parallelism (overridden by pool settings if you use them).

5. When to Tinker

- **Scaling Up:** As your deployment grows, you'll almost certainly need to adjust settings related to resource usage and your chosen executor.
- **Security:** If you're using Airflow in a sensitive environment, dive into its authentication options.
- **Fine-Tuning:** Want to change how frequently logs are rotated, or tweak UI colors? The config file awaits!

Practical Exercise

1. **Explore Your Config:** Open up your `airflow.cfg` file. Are there any default settings that immediately jump out at you as something you might need to change?
2. **Documentation is Your Friend:** Pick one setting that's unfamiliar from the list above, and look it up in Airflow's documentation. What are the use cases where adjusting it would make sense?

Additional Resources

- **Airflow Configuration Reference:**
  https://airflow.apache.org/docs/apache-airflow/stable/configurations-ref/index.html

Next Up: Let's explore the strengths and limitations of the SequentialExecutor, the simplest way to run your Airflow tasks

Sequential Strategy: Understanding the Sequential Executor

1. The Essence of Simplicity

The SequentialExecutor is the most basic of Airflow's executors. Key characteristics:

- **Single Process:** Tasks within a DAG run sequentially (one after the other), directly as part of the Scheduler process itself.
- **No Additional Setup:** If you just installed Airflow and did nothing special, this is likely what you're using by default.
- **Inherently Limited:** No parallelism whatsoever. If one task is slow, it blocks everything that comes after it in that DAG.

2. When is the SequentialExecutor the Right Tool?

- **Early Development:** When you're just sketching out the logic of your pipelines, it keeps things easy. You don't need worker nodes yet.
- **Small-Scale Pipelines:** If you only have a handful of tasks, and they execute reasonably quickly, the overhead of a distributed executor might be unnecessary.
- **Resource Constraints:** Maybe you're running Airflow on a tiny machine or in a limited environment where you can't spare resources for workers.

3. Beware the Pitfalls

- **Bottlenecks:** As soon as a single task becomes slow (network issues, large data processing), your entire DAG grinds to a halt.
- **No Scalability:** If your pipeline needs evolve, switching executors later is disruptive. Keep an eye on execution times during development.
- **Lack of Isolation:** A buggy task can potentially crash your entire Airflow Scheduler process.

4. Visualizing the SequentialExecutor

Think of it like a one-lane road:

- **Scheduler = Traffic Cop:** Directs the flow.
- **Tasks = Cars:** Each car must finish its journey before the next one can start.
- **Traffic Jams = Slow Tasks:** Hold up everyone in line.

5. When to Graduate

Consider switching executors if:

- **DAG runs are consistently slow.**
- **You want better resilience.** If the Scheduler process dies with the SequentialExecutor, in-progress tasks are lost.
- **You anticipate needing to process larger amounts of data, or tasks with high resource needs**

Practical Exercise

1. **Are You Using It?** Look at your Airflow configuration file. If you don't see an `executor` setting explicitly defined, you're on the SequentialExecutor!
2. **Can You Afford It?** Examine your DAGs' runtimes. Are there tasks that seem to be taking much longer than others, creating bottlenecks?

Additional Resources

- **Airflow Docs on the SequentialExecutor:**
  https://airflow.apache.org/docs/apache-airflow/stable/executor/sequential.html

Next Up: Let's explore Airflow's LocalExecutor, which introduces the ability to run tasks in parallel, still within a single machine.

Local Logic: Harnessing the Power of the LocalExecutor

1. Stepping Up Your Game

The LocalExecutor provides a convenient way to scale your Airflow deployment beyond the limitations of the SequentialExecutor. Key benefits include:

- **Parallelism (Within Limits):** By launching tasks as separate processes, the LocalExecutor enables a degree of concurrency, making better use of your machine's resources.
- **A Bit of Isolation:** If a single task crashes, it's less likely to bring down your entire Airflow Scheduler, improving the stability of your pipelines.
- **Still No Dedicated Workers:** Unlike a full-fledged Celery setup, the LocalExecutor manages all task execution directly on the same machine as your Scheduler and webserver.

2. When to Choose the LocalExecutor

Consider the LocalExecutor for the following scenarios:

- **Moderate Pipelines:** If you've outgrown the SequentialExecutor, the LocalExecutor lets you squeeze more performance from your existing hardware before needing a complex cluster setup.
- **Resource Constraints:** When you have a reasonably powerful single machine, and it's not practical or cost-effective to add separate worker nodes, the LocalExecutor lets you make the most of what you have.
- **Hybrid Deployments:** Airflow allows you to mix and match executors! The LocalExecutor is great for smaller or less critical DAGs, while you can reserve the power of Celery for your heaviest production workloads.

3. How It Works

Here's a breakdown of the LocalExecutor's mechanics:

- **Scheduler Forks Processes:** When it's time to run a task, the Scheduler forks a new process, providing a separate execution environment.
- **Configuration is Key:** Settings like `parallelism`, `max_active_tasks_per_dag`, and `pool` sizes offer granular control over how many tasks can run simultaneously and how resources are shared.
- **Resource Awareness:** While tasks run in separate processes, they still compete for CPU, memory, and other resources on your machine. Careful configuration is essential to avoid overloading.

4. The Balancing Act

The LocalExecutor offers a compelling middle ground, but it's important to be aware of its trade-offs:

- **Pros:**
    - More throughput than SequentialExecutor
    - Increased resilience compared to SequentialExecutor
    - Simple setup without the need for external workers
- **Cons:**
    - Ultimately, you're still limited by the capabilities of a single machine.
    - Overloading your machine risks negatively impacting the performance of Airflow's core components (Scheduler, webserver).
    - Tasks share the machine's environment, so conflicting dependencies or isolated resource requirements might be better handled by Celery's dedicated workers.

5. Considerations Before Switching

- **Task Resource Needs:** Analyze your DAGs. Do you have a small number of resource-intensive tasks, or many lightweight ones? The LocalExecutor is better suited to the latter, as a few heavy tasks could quickly overwhelm your machine.
- **Dependency Conflicts:** If your tasks require wildly different libraries, packages, or have conflicting versions, the LocalExecutor's shared environment might lead to issues. In this case, Celery's isolated workers provide a cleaner solution.
- **Future Growth:** Even if a powerful single machine suits your needs *now*, anticipate your pipeline's growth. Could you reach a point where the LocalExecutor becomes a bottleneck, requiring the flexibility of Celery?

Practical Exercise

1. **Resource Check:** Determine the specifications of the machine where your Airflow installation runs. How many CPU cores, available memory, and disk space do you have? This will directly inform the potential capacity of the LocalExecutor.

Additional Resources

- **Airflow Docs on the LocalExecutor:**
  https://airflow.apache.org/docs/apache-airflow/stable/executor/local.html

Next Up: Let's dive into the scalable and robust world of the CeleryExecutor

Celery Charm: Exploring the Celery Executor

1. The Power of Distributed Task Execution

Celery is a production-grade asynchronous task queue often used in Python web development. Its integration with Airflow unlocks the following for your pipelines:

- **Scalability:**
    - Introduce separate worker nodes to dramatically increase your DAGs' capacity.
    - Handle heavy workloads or a large number of concurrent tasks.
- **Resilience:**
    - Workers are independent – one crashing doesn't bring down your whole system.
    - Celery can retry failed tasks, improving pipeline robustness.
- **Resource Isolation:**
    - Assign workers dedicated hardware (great for heavy tasks, specialized dependencies, or GPUs!).
    - Manage workloads that wouldn't play nice on a single shared machine.

2. How the CeleryExecutor Works

Let's break down the dance between Airflow and Celery:

1. **Scheduler:** Instead of directly executing a task, the Scheduler puts a message describing the task onto a Celery queue.
2. **Broker:** A message broker (like RabbitMQ or Redis) acts as the intermediary, reliably storing and routing these task messages.
3. **Workers:** Celery worker nodes constantly listen to the queue. When a worker picks up a message, it executes the corresponding Airflow task.
4. **Results:** Celery communicates results back to the broker, which Airflow then retrieves to update the task's state in the UI and metadata database.

3. Setting Up a Celery Deployment

The essentials to get started:

1. **Choose a Broker:** RabbitMQ and Redis are popular options.
2. **Configure Airflow:** Set `executor = CeleryExecutor` in your `airflow.cfg` and point to your broker's URL.

3. **Spin Up Workers:** Run `airflow celery worker` on one or more machines. The more workers you have, the more tasks you can execute in parallel.

4. When Celery Shines

Consider the CeleryExecutor a necessity if you encounter the following:

- **Performance Bottlenecks:** The LocalExecutor is maxing out your machine, and tasks are taking too long to complete.
- **High Resource Needs:** Your DAGs include tasks with significant CPU, memory, or GPU demands.
- **Strict Isolation:** Tasks have conflicting dependencies, or security is a top priority.
- **Anticipated Growth:** You foresee that your data pipelines will need to scale significantly over time.

5. Considerations & Cautions

- **Added Complexity:** Managing a distributed system introduces overhead – you'll need to monitor workers and the broker itself.
- **Communication Overhead:** The back-and-forth between Airflow and Celery has latency. Simple tasks may run slightly slower compared to a LocalExecutor setup.
- **Potential for Errors:** Be sure to have robust error handling and retry mechanisms as message passing introduces extra failure points.

Practical Exercise

1. **Do You Need It?** Analyze your most demanding DAG. Consider the runtime, resource needs, the importance of finishing quickly, and whether running in isolation is important for stability.
2. **Broker Options:** If you're not already using one, research RabbitMQ vs. Redis for your use case. What are the trade-offs?

Additional Resources

- **Airflow CeleryExecutor Docs:** https://airflow.apache.org/docs/apache-airflow/stable/executor/celery/index.html
- **Celery Project Website:** https://docs.celeryproject.org/en/stable/index.html

Next Up: Let's explore how Airflow's configuration settings allow you to fine-tune your deployment, getting the most out of your chosen executor!

Config Clarity: Navigating Current Configuration

1. The Importance of a Well-Configured Airflow

- **Performance:** Settings that control resource usage and task execution directly impact how efficiently your pipelines run.
- **Behavior:** Airflow's flexibility comes from its configurability. Understanding it grants you precise control over scheduling, retries, how it interacts with external systems, etc.
- **Troubleshooting:** When things go wrong, knowing where configuration values are set and what they mean is the first step in diagnosing problems.

2. Where Settings Reside

1. **The `airflow.cfg` File:**
   - The heart of your Airflow configuration.
   - Structured into sections (e.g., `[core]`, `[scheduler]`)
   - Each section has key-value pairs to adjust settings.
2. **Environment Variables:**
   - Can override certain things in your `airflow.cfg`
   - Prefixed with `AIRFLOW__` (e.g., `AIRFLOW__CORE__EXECUTOR=CeleryExecutor`)
3. **DAG-level:**
   - Parameters like `max_active_tasks_per_dag`, `concurrency`, etc., let you tailor how specific DAGs behave within your broader Airflow environment.

3. Key Configuration Areas to Know

(Important: This won't be an exhaustive list of every setting, but a highlight of important ones.)

- **Executor Settings (`[core]`)**
  - `executor`: Sequential, Local, Celery, Kubernetes... this is fundamental
  - `parallelism`, `core__dag_concurrency` and related settings, shape how much work can happen at once.
- **Database (`[core]`)**
  - `sql_alchemy_conn`: Where Airflow stores metadata (task status, history, etc.).
- **Webserver (`[webserver]`)**

- UI appearance, authentication options, how many items are displayed per page…
- **Celery ([celery]) (If you use the CeleryExecutor)**
  - `broker_url`: How Airflow finds your task queue
  - `celeryd_concurrency`: How many tasks a single worker can handle at once

4. Deciphering Defaults vs. Changes

- **Fresh Install:** Airflow ships with a default `airflow.cfg`. These values are a sensible starting place, but likely need adjustment as you scale up.
- **Spotting Modifications:** Comparing your `airflow.cfg` to a clean default helps identify what you've customized, which is vital when upgrading Airflow versions or doing deep troubleshooting.

5. Tips for Effective Configuration Management

- **Document, Document!** Comment your `airflow.cfg` explaining *why* certain settings are chosen, not just what they are.
- **Version Control:** Treat `airflow.cfg` like code. Track changes over time using a system like Git.
- **Environment-Specific Config:** For complex setups, maintain separate configuration files for development, staging, and production environments.
- **Overrides with Care:** Environment variables are tempting for quick fixes, but overusing them makes your configuration harder to track as a whole.

Practical Exercise

1. **Explore Your Settings:** Open your `airflow.cfg` file. Identify 3 settings you don't recognize. Look them up in the Airflow Documentation to understand their purpose. Are the current values appropriate for how you use Airflow?

Additional Resources

- **Airflow Configuration Reference:**
  https://airflow.apache.org/docs/apache-airflow/stable/reference/configurations-ref.html
- **Managing Airflow Configurations (Blog post):**
  https://towardsdatascience.com/managing-airflow-configurations-using-environment-variables-and-config-files-ee5a88dbf792

Next Up: Let's explore how Airflow allows you to run your DAGs in parallel, significantly improving performance!

Parallel Prowess: Adding Parallel DAGs to Your Repository

1. Why Parallelism Matters

As your data pipelines grow, sequential execution might become a bottleneck. Parallelism lets you:

- **Speed Up Execution:** Tasks that can run independently do so simultaneously, shortening the total time your DAG takes to finish.
- **Maximize Resource Usage:** Make the most of your hardware (especially with the LocalExecutor or CeleryExecutor) by not letting CPU cores or worker nodes sit idle.
- **Logical Organization:** In some cases, breaking a large process into clean parallel steps improves DAG readability.

2. Designing for Parallelism

Not everything is a perfect fit for parallelization. Ask yourself:

- **True Independence:** Can tasks *actually* run simultaneously without conflicts, race conditions, or one task needing another's output?
- **Resource Contention:** If parallel tasks all heavily use the same resource (database, network), you might not see actual gains.
- **Cost vs. Benefit:** If a DAG is already fast, the overhead of introducing parallelism might not be worth it.

3. Techniques for Parallel Execution

1. **Within a DAG:** Airflow Operators themselves orchestrate tasks. By designing your DAG structure cleverly, independent branches can proceed simultaneously.
2. **Multiple DAGs (with Caveats):**
   - It's tempting to run entirely separate DAGs concurrently. However, Airflow by default has global resource limits (across all DAGs).
   - Effective if you have a few large DAGs, but loses granularity of control.

4. Key Configuration Settings

These settings live primarily in your `airflow.cfg` file:

- `core.parallelism`: Global maximum for how many tasks Airflow can run at once, across *all* DAGs.
- `core.dag_concurrency`: Maximum concurrent tasks within a *single* DAG.

- **DAG-level `max_active_tasks_per_dag`:** Overrides the core setting for a specific DAG to tailor its limits.
- **Pool Settings:** Using pools, you add finer control, reserving resources for certain types of tasks.

5. Parallelism in Practice

Scenario: You process files uploaded by users. Each file's processing is independent of others.

Strategy:

- **Single DAG:** One DAG with a task to 'fan out', launching a processing sub-task dynamically for each file detected.
- **Dynamic DAGs:** A pattern where your code *generates* separate DAGs on the fly, one per file (more advanced).

Practical Exercise

1. **Spot the Bottlenecks:** Analyze your slowest DAGs in the Airflow UI. Is the slowness due to sequential tasks that *could* run independently?
2. **Estimate the Gains:** If you restructured a DAG for parallelism, considering your hardware setup, roughly how much faster do you think it would realistically run?

Next Up: Let's explore Flower, the powerful tool to monitor your task execution within Airflow!

Task Transparency: Monitoring Tasks with Flower

1. Why Flower Matters

Airflow's own UI, while valuable, has limitations:

- **Task-Level Focus:** It can be cumbersome to get a quick real-time overview of task states (running, failed, succeeded) across multiple DAGs.
- **Historical Limitations:** Airflow's UI primarily shows recent runs. Analyzing longer-term trends can be difficult.
- **Worker Health (Celery):** Basic worker status is visible, but Flower offers more detail.

2. Enter Flower

Flower is a separate web application designed specifically for monitoring Celery, and hence Airflow when you use the CeleryExecutor. Key features:

- **Dashboard:** A clean, real-time view of tasks in progress, their states, and start/end times for every DAG run.
- **Worker Monitoring:** See which workers are online, their load, detailed task queue status, etc.
- **Historical Information:** Browse past task and DAG runs, filter by state – invaluable for debugging.
- **Grid View:** Shows task execution times for multiple runs at once, helping pinpoint consistently slow tasks.

3. Setting Up Flower

1. **Installation:** Typically `pip install flower`
2. **Launch:** Run the `flower` command, providing your Airflow's Celery broker URL as an argument.
3. **Access:** Flower runs a web server; access it in your browser (e.g., http://localhost:5555).

4. Using Flower Effectively

- **The Task List:** Your home base. See active/failed tasks, retry attempts, and get links to the Airflow UI logs of specific tasks.
- **Worker View:**
    - Spot overwhelmed or offline workers.
    - For long tasks, sometimes you can see them queued up, awaiting an available worker.

- **Historical Analysis:** Notice a task failing consistently at the same time of day? That might hint towards an external dependency problem.

5. Considerations

- **Security:** In production, don't expose Flower publicly. Put it behind authentication or limit access to within your internal network.
- **Resource Usage:** Flower, especially with historical data, uses its own database. Ensure it's appropriately sized for your Airflow deployment.
- **It's a Companion:** Flower excels at task and worker monitoring, but doesn't replace the Airflow UI for configuring DAGs or editing code.

Practical Exercise

1. **Flower Installation:** If you haven't already, install and run Flower connected to your Airflow setup.
2. **Task Observation:** Trigger a DAG run. Watch as tasks change states in Flower's interface. Can you correlate what you see with how the DAG is visualized in Airflow's Graph View?

Additional Resources

- **Flower Project Website:** https://flower.readthedocs.io/en/latest/
- **Guide to Using Flower with Airflow:** https://airflow.apache.org/docs/apache-airflow/stable/ui.html#flower-monitoring-tool

Next Up: Let's streamline your Airflow setup by removing the example DAGs that come by default.

Streamlining: Removing Default DAG Examples

1. Why Remove the Example DAGs?

While a helpful starting point, the default Airflow DAGs serve a few key purposes but ultimately outlive their usefulness quickly. Here's why it's wise to clear them out:

- **Reduce Confusion:** Newcomers to Airflow might mistake these examples as core parts of how to build production pipelines, leading to less-than-ideal patterns.
- **Cleanliness is Key:** Unnecessary DAGs clutter your UI, making it harder to find your own work.
- **Performance (Slight):** While minimal, Airflow does expend some resources parsing and loading even inactive DAGs. In large setups, this can add up.

2. The Safe Removal Process

Fear not – deleting the default DAGs won't break anything in Airflow itself. Here's the proper way to do it:

1. **Locate Your `dags_folder`:** Find the directory where Airflow looks for DAG files. You likely specified this in your `airflow.cfg`.
2. **Identify the Culprits:** Default DAG filenames typically start with `example_`. There will likely be several Python (.py) files.
3. **Delete:** Use your operating system's file manager to simply delete these example DAG files.
4. **Restart Airflow:** For the changes to take effect, restart the Airflow webserver and Scheduler processes.

3. Best Practices: Examples as a Learning Tool

Rather than outright deletion, consider these alternatives for beginners:

- **Temporary Move:** Move the example files to a different folder *outside* your `dags_folder`. You can reference them later without them cluttering Airflow.
- **Create an 'Archive':** Within your `dags_folder`, make a subdirectory like `archive` and move the example DAGs into it. Airflow will ignore them there, but you retain a reference.
- **Version Control:** If using Git (and you should be!), commit the original examples, then delete them locally. You can always revert with Git if needed.

4. Beyond the Basics: Structuring Your Own DAGs

With the examples gone, use this opportunity to think about your ideal Airflow project structure:

- **Logical Grouping:** Should you create subfolders within `dags_folder` for different domains (marketing pipelines, ETL processes, etc.)?
- **File Naming:** Establish clear conventions (e.g., `department_process_name_dag.py`) to make finding DAGs easy as your project grows.

Practical Exercise

1. **Out with the Old:** If you haven't already, remove the default DAGs using a method you're comfortable with.
2. **DAG Housekeeping:** Do any of your own DAGs have unclear names or seem like they could be reorganized? This is a good time to do some tidying!

Additional Resources

- **Airflow Docs on DAG Loading:**
  https://airflow.apache.org/docs/apache-airflow/stable/concepts/dags.html#loading-dags

Next Up: Let's explore how Celery workers are the engines that turn your DAGs into reality!

Worker Wonders: Running Tasks on Celery Workers

1. Workers: Where the Magic Happens

Let's break down the relationship between the core Airflow components and the Celery workers:

- **Scheduler:** Your DAG mastermind. It determines *what* needs to be done and *when*.
- **Message Queue (Broker):** Using technologies like RabbitMQ, this acts as the organized inbox of tasks waiting to be executed.
- **Workers:** Independent processes that listen to the queue, receive task instructions, and carry them out. It's here that the code within your Operators actually runs.

2. Why Celery Workers Matter

They are essential for scaling Airflow beyond the limitations of a single machine:

- **True Parallelism:** Each worker is a separate process and can pick up new tasks while others are still busy. The more workers (often on different machines), the more your capacity grows.
- **Resource Specialization:** Need tasks that use GPUs? Tasks that need odd libraries? Deploy workers on machines tailored for specific needs.
- **Fault Tolerance:** If a worker crashes mid-task, Celery has mechanisms for detecting this and the task can be retried, often by a different worker.

3. Setting Up Workers

The essentials:

1. **Provision Machines:** These could be additional physical servers, virtual machines, or even containers.
2. **Install Celery:** Ensure Celery is installed on each worker machine.
3. **Point to the Broker:** Workers need the same broker URL (in your `airflow.cfg`) as your main Airflow installation.
4. **Launch:** Use the `airflow celery worker` command. You'll see the worker connect to the queue and announce it's ready.

4. Celery Workers in Action: Visualizing the Action

The beauty of this setup is visible within Airflow's UI:

- **Task State Changes:** As workers pick up tasks, you'll see tasks transition from 'queued' to 'running' in almost real-time.
- **Worker Logs:** The logs for a task execution now live on the worker machine Airflow's UI links to those logs for debugging.
- **Flower Monitoring:** Flower gives you a detailed view of worker status, their task load, and even allows you to shutdown workers gracefully.

5. Considerations and Optimizations

- **Worker Sizing:** How much CPU/memory should each worker have? This mirrors sizing any machine that runs your typical data pipeline tasks.
- **Concurrency Settings:** Each worker can handle multiple tasks at once. `celeryd_concurrency` in Airflow's configuration and your chosen pool settings affect this.
- **Autoscaling:** Cloud environments often let you add/remove workers based on demand. This is a powerful level for making your Airflow setup cost-effective.

Practical Exercise

1. **Worker Check:** If you use Celery, can you find the hostname of the machine(s) your Celery workers are running on by looking at completed tasks in the Airflow UI?
2. **Resource Awareness:** Think of a task in a DAG. Does it require a lot of memory? A specialized dependency? Would it benefit from having a dedicated worker provisioned for it?

Additional Resources

- **Celery Distributed Task Queue Website:**
  https://docs.celeryproject.org/en/stable/
- **Apache Airflow Documentation on CeleryExecutor:**
  https://airflow.apache.org/docs/apache-airflow/stable/executor/celery.html

Next Up: Let's explore message queues, the backbone that allows communication between Airflow components and your workers.

Queue Queries: Understanding the Essence of Queues

1. Message Queues: The Organized Inbox

Think of a message queue in Airflow (and distributed systems generally) like a very structured inbox with special rules:

- **Producers:** The Airflow Scheduler puts task descriptions on the queue.
- **Consumers:** Celery workers pull tasks off the queue in the order received.
- **Message Durability:** Good queue technologies ensure that even if something crashes, messages aren't lost.
- **Reliability:** Messages should be processed once (and only once) for data pipeline integrity.

2. Why Queues are Crucial to Airflow

1. **Decoupling:** The Scheduler doesn't directly hand off work to workers. This allows you to easily scale workers and the Scheduler independently.
2. **Buffering:** If your workers are temporarily overwhelmed, the queue absorbs the backlog, letting them catch up when they can.
3. **Resilience:** If the Scheduler process restarts, the queue preserves tasks in progress. Similarly, a worker crash doesn't cause the task itself to vanish.

3. Popular Message Queue Options

- **RabbitMQ:** A mature, robust message broker. A common choice for Airflow.
- **Redis:** Technically more of an in-memory data store, but can be used as a simple and fast message queue.
- **Amazon SQS, Kafka:** Options if you're heavily invested in those cloud platforms, or need the scale they offer.

4. "Talking" to the Queue

While you won't usually interact with the message queue directly, understanding these concepts helps with troubleshooting:

- **Enqueueing:** Airflow's act of putting a task message onto the queue.
- **Dequeueing:** A Celery worker grabbing a message and marking it as 'in progress'
- **Message Acknowledgement:** After the worker **successfully** completes the task, it tells the queue the message can be removed.
- **Retries:** If a worker fails, the task may become available again after a timeout, depending on queue settings.

5. Queues as a Monitoring Tool

Even without looking at the queue's own interface, Airflow hints at its state:

- **Tasks Stuck in 'Queued' State:** This could mean no workers are running, or the queue itself can't be reached.
- **Flower's Worker View:** Shows what tasks are in progress on which worker, and if Celery thinks the queue is lagging.

Practical Exercise

1. **Broker Settings:** Check your `airflow.cfg`. What's the `broker_url` set to? This tells you both your message queue technology and how to connect to it.
2. **Thinking Critically:** Could something be misconfigured if tasks get 'stuck' immediately upon running, even if workers seem to be online? (Hint: Is the Airflow Scheduler's idea of the queue the same as the workers'?)

Additional Resources

- **RabbitMQ Website:** https://www.rabbitmq.com/
- **Redis Website:** https://redis.io/
- **Celery's Result Backend Settings:** (These can use the same technologies as the main broker):
  https://docs.celeryproject.org/en/stable/userguide/configuration.html#result-backend

Next Up: Let's explore how to add another Celery worker to increase the muscle of your Airflow deployment!

Expanding Capacity: Adding a New Celery Worker

1. Why Add More Workers?

Several scenarios might call for expanding your workforce:

- **Hitting Limits:** Are tasks frequently stuck in the 'queued' state for extended periods, even when your current worker seems idle?
- **Scaling Up Workload:** Are you anticipating a significant increase in the number or complexity of your DAGs?
- **Specialized Tasks:** Do you have certain tasks that need to run on machines with unique hardware or software resources?

2. Preparation is Key

Before spinning up the worker, ensure these basics are in place:

1. **Provisioning:** Do you have an additional machine – a physical server, virtual machine, or even a container – ready to become the new worker?
2. **Airflow Access:** Is Airflow itself installed and configured on this new machine?
3. **Shared Environment:**
    - **Code:** Can the worker access the same DAG files as your other Airflow components?
    - **Configuration:** Does it have the same `airflow.cfg` settings, crucially the same broker URL, pointing to the same message queue.

3. The Worker Launch Process

The good news: launching a new worker is remarkably simple!

1. **On the Worker Machine:** Make sure Celery is installed (`pip install celery`).
2. **The Magic Command:** From the command line, initiate the worker process: `airflow celery worker`
3. **Observe:**
    - The worker will log its connection to the queue.
    - In Airflow's UI, if you have Flower running, a new worker node should appear.
    - Tasks should begin to be scheduled onto this new worker!

4. Important Considerations

- **Naming:** While optional, if you launch multiple workers on a single machine, it's wise to give them names: `airflow celery worker -n worker2`. This helps with monitoring.
- **Auto-Scaling (Advanced):** Cloud environments often allow virtual machine groups to expand/shrink based on demand. This automation aligns your Airflow costs with the actual workload.
- **Resource Limits:** How much RAM/CPU each worker gets may influence how *many* workers you need. More powerful individual workers vs. a larger swarm is a trade-off to explore.

5. When More Workers Might NOT Help

Watch out for bottlenecks elsewhere that a new worker won't fix:

- **Database Overload:** If your task executions heavily interact with a database, it might be the database that's the limiting factor.
- **Scheduler Throughput:** A single Airflow Scheduler can become overwhelmed if your number of DAGs grows too large.
- **Network Limits:** Tasks that move large amounts of data can be constrained by network speeds.

Practical Exercise

1. **How Many Now?** Take a peek at your Airflow Flower interface. How many workers do you currently have running?
2. **Resource Check:** Consider a new DAG you'd like to add to your Airflow deployment. Estimate its memory and CPU usage at peak. Could your current worker setup comfortably absorb this additional load?

Additional Resources

- **Celery Flower Documentation:** https://flower.readthedocs.io/en/latest/

Next Up: Let's explore strategies to optimize how Airflow distributes tasks among your pool of workers, using queues!

Queue Management: Optimizing Task Distribution

1. Queues: Not Just a Waiting Line

While Celery workers pull tasks off queues in a mostly sequential manner, Airflow adds an extra layer of sophistication with its concept of pools and priority weights:

- **Pools:** Think of these as named buckets of resources. Tasks can get assigned to a specific pool. Each pool has a slot limit (how many tasks can run concurrently from that pool).
- **Priority Weights:** Not only can you put a task in a pool, but within that pool, it gets a priority score. Higher priority tasks will be picked up by workers *ahead* of lower priority ones, even if they were queued earlier.

2. Why Queue Management Matters

Naive usage of queues can lead to problems:

- **Starvation:** Low-priority but important tasks might never run if the queues are always full of high-priority ones.
- **Resource Mismatch:** You might have workers dedicated to GPU tasks, but the queues are sending those workers simple text processing tasks.
- **Under-utilization:** Too many pools with small limits can artificially prevent tasks from running in parallel, even if there is capacity.

3. Queue Configuration in Practice

Let's look at where you control queues in Airflow:

- **airflow.cfg:**
    - The `celery_pool` setting can provide a default pool for tasks
- **DAG Level:** Within your DAG definition, parameters like `pool` and `priority_weight` affect where each task will try to land.
- **Operator Level (Less Common):** Individual operators sometimes have pool-related arguments to override the DAG default.
- **Airflow UI (Ad-hoc):** When manually triggering a task run, you can sometimes select its pool dynamically.

4. Smart Queue Strategies

Here's how to use pools and priorities to your advantage:

- **Critical Path Isolation:** If a task is on the critical path of your DAG (blocking many others), give it a dedicated pool and a high priority, ensuring it gets executed quickly.
- **Tiered Workloads:** "Gold", "Silver", and "Bronze" pools could reflect batch jobs that can run overnight vs. user-facing tasks needing immediate attention.
- **Hardware Matching:** Pools named after worker types (`gpu_pool`, `high_memory_pool`) guide tasks to the right machines.
- **Enforcing Fairness:** Task priority should be used with care, but can prevent a few very heavy tasks from permanently clogging the queues.

5. Monitoring Your Queues

Tools to help you understand what's *really* happening with your task distribution:

- **Airflow UI – Pool View:** Shows slots used vs. total for each pool.
- **Flower:** Gives detailed worker views, including what tasks from which pools are currently running or queued on each worker.

Practical Exercise

1. **Pool Audit:** List the pools currently defined in your Airflow setup (check your `airflow.cfg` and look at a few DAG definitions). Are their names and slot limits sensible?
2. **DAG Priorities:** Pick your most complex DAG. Do the task priorities within it make logical sense given the dependencies in its graph structure?

Additional Resources

- **Airflow Documentation: Pools:**
  https://airflow.apache.org/docs/apache-airflow/stable/concepts/pools.html
- **Airflow Priority Weights:**
  https://airflow.apache.org/docs/apache-airflow/stable/concepts/priority-and-queue.html#priority-weight

Next Up: Let's explore how to target tasks to specific Celery queues or workers for specialized execution needs

Targeted Tasks: Directing Tasks to Specific Queues

1. When the Default Queue Isn't Enough

Standard Airflow behavior sends tasks to a queue based on their pool settings. But there are times you need more direct control:

- **Special Workers:** You might have workers with unique hardware or software that only a few tasks should ever use.
- **Critical Isolation:** A task so important and time-sensitive that you want to create a queue exclusively for it.
- **Experimental Workloads:** Testing a new Operator type and don't want to risk it interfering with production traffic.
- **Troubleshooting:** To isolate problematic tasks and prevent them from clogging up your main queues.

2. Mechanisms for Targeting

Airflow gives you a couple of ways to override the default queue a task lands in:

- **Operator Level:** Many Operators accept a `queue` argument. This is the most precise way to target.
- **DAG Level:** The less frequently used `default_queue` parameter during DAG creation sets a fallback queue for tasks within it.

3. Important Considerations

- **Worker Knowledge:** Workers must be configured to listen to the specific queues you'll be targeting. Otherwise, tasks routed there will languish.
- **Pool and Queue Harmony:** Often, it's wise to pair a task sent to a custom queue with also assigning it to a unique pool to ensure resources are carved out specifically for those tasks.
- **Visibility:** Flower is your best tool for monitoring non-standard queues. Queues not actively being listened to by workers will still show up in its interface!

4. Example Scenario: GPU Intensive Tasks

Let's say you have:

- **Workers with GPUs:** Marked by being in the `gpu_pool`.
- **GPU-heavy Tasks:** A subset of your data processing Operators that leverage TensorFlow, PyTorch, etc.

Your Configuration:

- `special_gpu_queue`: Create a new queue.
- **Worker Config:** Ensure your GPU workers are configured to listen to both your normal queues and `special_gpu_queue`.
- **Operator Arguments:** On your GPU tasks, set `queue='special_gpu_queue'`.

Now, those tasks will bypass standard routing and reliably end up on your capable machines.

5. Queue Targeting in Practice

- **Reasoning is Key:** Don't target queues without purpose. It adds complexity. Document *why* certain tasks are being given special treatment.
- **Balance with Pools:** Use queues and pools in tandem for the most effective management of worker resources.

Practical Exercise

1. **Queue Checkup:** Can you find an example in your own Airflow setup (if using Celery) where a task is explicitly assigned to a non-default queue?
2. **Hypothetical:** Imagine you add a new task type that heavily depends on network speed. Would a custom queue make sense in that scenario? Why or why not?

Additional Resources

- **Airflow Docs on Celery Executor**
  https://airflow.apache.org/docs/apache-airflow/stable/executor/celery.html

Concurrency Concepts: Mastering Crucial Parameters for Efficiency

1. Concurrency: The Big Picture

Concurrency in Airflow is about how many tasks can be actively running *at the same time*. This has multiple layers:

- **Global:** Airflow itself has limits to safeguard against overloading your system
- **DAG Level:** Each DAG can throttle how many of its own tasks run in parallel.
- **Worker Level:** Individual Celery workers have a cap on concurrent tasks.
- **Pool Limits:** Task slots within pools further restrict how resources are used.

2. Key Configuration Settings

These are the knobs you'll primarily be tuning in your `airflow.cfg` file:

- `core.parallelism`: The absolute maximum tasks Airflow will run across *all* your DAGs at once. This is your failsafe.
- `core.dag_concurrency`: Limits how many tasks from a single DAG can be running simultaneously.
- `celery.worker_concurrency`: Sets how many tasks a single worker will take on at max.
- **Pool Settings:** Each pool has a `slots` setting

3. When to Adjust Concurrency

Reasons to consider changes from the defaults:

- **Hitting Walls:** Are tasks frequently 'queued' but not starting? This often (but not always) indicates you could raise some limits.
- **Resource Exhaustion:** If database connections, network, or the workers themselves are overwhelmed, you might need to *lower* concurrency.
- **Fairness:** Prevent a few very 'wide' DAGs from hogging all task slots, starving other parts of your system.
- **Cost Control:** Especially in cloud environments, concurrency can directly correlate to the cost of running your Airflow setup.

4. Interactions Between Settings

It's crucial to realize these settings work together:

1. **A Task Needs a Worker:** Even if your DAG and pools would allow a task to run, it won't start unless a worker has a free slot.

2. **DAG Concurrency is per DAG:** If you set `dag_concurrency=5`, a single DAG could have 5 tasks active, even if your `parallelism` is lower.
3. **Pools Add a Layer:** Task slots within a pool further limit what can run, even if the DAG and worker have capacity.

5. Monitoring the Symphony (or Bottlenecks)

- **Airflow UI:**
    - The DAGs view shows a concurrency column.
    - Gantt charts visually reveal tasks waiting for slots to open up.
- **Flower:** Examine which workers are at capacity and which have room to spare.

Practical Exercise

1. **Know Your Limits:** What's the current `parallelism` setting for your Airflow installation? Could you safely increase it given your hardware?
2. **Spot the Bottleneck:** Can you find a DAG where tasks get stuck in the 'queued' state for longer than seems reasonable? What concurrency settings might be the culprit?

Additional Resources

- **Airflow Docs: Configuration Options**
    https://airflow.apache.org/docs/apache-airflow/stable/configurations-ref.html

Section 7:
Mastering Advanced Airflow Techniques

Bidding Farewell to Repetitive Patterns: Streamlining Workflow Structures

1. The Problem with Redundant DAGs

As your organization's use of Airflow matures, you might find yourself in these situations:

- **Copy-Paste Proliferation:** DAGs that are very similar, differing only in minor tweaks to data sources or parameters.
- **Tetris Logic:** Complex dependencies leading to chains of DAGs with hard-coded schedules to trigger them in sequence.
- **Hardcoded Everything:** DAGs littered with values that should be centrally managed as configuration.

This leads to maintenance headaches and the risk of inconsistencies creeping in!

2. Strategies for Simplification

Airflow provides tools to combat this complexity:

- **Templating:** Inject parameters into your DAGs at runtime. A single DAG can then serve multiple purposes. See Jinja templating within your Operator definitions.
- **Providers:** Abstract away connections to common services (S3, cloud databases, SaaS APIs). Operators within your DAGs then reference these providers, keeping your DAG code cleaner.
- **External Configuration:** Store database connection strings, thresholds, or even the targets of data processing in a system outside Airflow (environment variables, a configuration file, a database).
- **Dynamic DAGs:** Python logic to generate DAG structures on the fly, ideal when elements of your pipelines are data-driven.

3. SubDAGs to the Rescue

A powerful weapon in your streamlining arsenal is the SubDAG. Think of it like a function call within your workflow:

- **Encapsulation:** Bundle a chunk of frequently repeated tasks into a SubDAG.
- **Reusability:** Use that same SubDAG across multiple parent DAGs, reducing redundancy.
- **Clarity:** The Graph View of your parent DAGs becomes much cleaner, showing the high-level flow rather than every minute step.

4. Example: User Acquisition Processing

Let's say you have these common steps in several DAGs:

1. Extract raw user signup data from a source
2. Clean and normalize the user data
3. Load the cleaned data into a reporting database

SubDAG Strategy:

- Create a `user_acquisition_processing.py` file defining a SubDAG containing those 3 tasks.
- In your main DAGs, use the `SubDagOperator` to invoke this reusable chunk of logic, passing in any source-specific parameters.

5. Considerations & Cautions

- **SubDAGs Aren't Magic:** They improve organization, but won't fix fundamentally inefficient tasks.
- **Balance:** Excessively small SubDAGs add overhead. Find the right level of granularity.
- **Version Control:** If SubDAGs are shared, consider them like libraries and manage their updates thoughtfully.

Practical Exercise

1. **Redundancy Audit:** Look at your most complex DAGs. Are there blocks of tasks that appear in multiple places? Could those be candidates to become SubDAGs?
2. **Parameter Search:** Are there values (like dates, bucket names, thresholds) hardcoded in your DAGs that would be better managed externally?

Additional Resources

- **Airflow Docs on SubDAGs:**
  https://airflow.apache.org/docs/apache-airflow/stable/concepts/dags/subdags.html

- **Airflow Docs on Dynamic DAGs:**
  https://airflow.apache.org/docs/apache-airflow/stable/concepts/dags/dynamic.html

Next Up: Let's explore how to group related tasks more flexibly using a feature simply called 'Task Groups'

Introducing Group Dynamics: Incorporating DAG Grouping for Efficiency

1. The Challenge of DAG Sprawl

As your use of Airflow grows, these problems might start creeping in:

- **Overly Complex Graph View:** The visual representation of your DAGs becomes a tangle of tasks, making it hard to understand the high-level structure.
- **UI Overload:** The DAGs list gets huge, making it difficult to find what you need.
- **Mental Model Mismatch:** Your mental image of the pipeline's steps may not cleanly align with how those steps are split across multiple DAGs due to technical limitations.

2. Enter Task Groups

Task Groups are *primarily* an organizational tool. Here's what they provide:

- **Nesting:** Define groups within your DAG. These groups show up visually collapsed in the Graph View, making things much neater.
- **UI Grouping:** Airflow's interface lets you filter and view DAGs by their group prefixes, taming a long list of DAGs.
- **No Execution Magic:** Tasks within a group still execute according to standard Airflow dependency rules. A group is like a visually pleasing fence drawn around sections of your process.

3. When to Use Task Groups

- **Logical Segmentation:** When a DAG has distinct phases (extract, transform, load), Task Groups mirror that structure.
- **Team-Based Views:** If different teams own parts of the pipeline, groups can be named to reflect that ownership.
- **Focusing Attention:** Collapse Task Groups that are currently unimportant, letting you zero in on a specific area of your DAG.

4. Task Groups in Action: Example

Let's say your DAG processes social media data:

1. **Tasks Without Grouping:**

- fetch_tweets
- extract_sentiment
- calculate_trends
- store_daily_report

2. **With Task Groups**

```
with TaskGroup("data_collection") as data_collection_group:
    fetch_tweets = ...
    extract_sentiment = ...

with TaskGroup("analysis") as analysis_group:
    calculate_trends = ...

store_daily_report = ...
```

5. Considerations

- **Not a Replacement for SubDAGs:** If you need reusability or to parameterize a whole chunk of logic, SubDAGs are still the way to go.
- **Cross-Group Dependencies:** Tasks in one group **can** depend on tasks in another. Airflow's dependency logic works as usual.
- **Nesting is Possible:** Task Groups can be nested within each other to create hierarchical organization.

Practical Exercise

1. **Group Audit:** Look at your largest DAG. Are there obvious sections that could be turned into Task Groups to improve its readability?
2. **Hypothetical:** If you were to add several new DAGs related to a single business process, how might Task Group prefixes help manage them in the Airflow UI?

Additional Resources

- **Airflow Docs on Task Groups:**
  https://airflow.apache.org/docs/apache-airflow/stable/concepts/task-groups.html

Next Up: Let's see how the SubDAG concept lets you encapsulate and reuse chunks of your Airflow pipelines!

SubDAG Simplified: Harnessing the Power of SubDAGs

1. Why SubDAGs Matter

As your Airflow DAGs become complex, SubDAGs help combat that complexity by:

- **Encapsulation:** Bundle a series of related tasks into a reusable mini-DAG.
- **Abstraction:** Your high-level DAGs become visually cleaner, with SubDAGs representing entire stages of your process.
- **Parameterization:** Pass data into and out of a SubDAG, making them function like code blocks.
- **Testing:** Develop and test complex segments of logic in isolation within their own SubDAG.

2. Creating a SubDAG

Treat a SubDAG almost like a standard DAG file:

1. **Separate File:** Place your SubDAG definition in its own .py file for organization.
2. **SubDagOperator:** In your 'parent' DAG, use the SubDagOperator to invoke your SubDAG.
3. **DAG ID:** Both your main DAG *and* the SubDAG need unique dag_id values.
4. **Parameters:** The SubDagOperator lets you pass arguments into the SubDAG if needed.

3. Example: Enhanced User Processing

Let's imagine this simplified parent DAG:

```python
from airflow import DAG
from airflow.operators.python import PythonOperator
from airflow.utils.dates import days_ago

with DAG(
    dag_id='main_user_dag',
    start_date=days_ago(1),
    schedule_interval="@daily"
) as dag:

    fetch_users = PythonOperator(task_id='fetch_users', ...)
```

```
    process_users = SubDagOperator(
        task_id='process_users',
subdag=create_user_processing_subdag('main_user_dag.process_us
ers')
    )

    store_results = PythonOperator(task_id='store_results',
...)

    fetch_users >> process_users >> store_results
```

Inside our `create_user_processing_subdag` function (in a separate file) would be the definition of the tasks that handle cleaning, transforming, and analyzing the user data.

4. Key Considerations

- **Dependency Hell? No!** Airflow handles dependencies between tasks in the main DAG and those within SubDAGs seamlessly.
- **Monitoring:** The Airflow UI shows the SubDAG expanded in the Graph View, letting you drill down into its execution.
- **SubDAGs of SubDAGs:** Yes, they can be nested! Use wisely, as overly deep nesting can hurt readability.
- **Not Just for Organization:** SubDAGs open up techniques like dynamically generating parts of your workflow.

5. When to Use SubDAGs vs. Other Techniques

- **Redundant Logic:** If you find yourself copying and pasting between DAGs, a SubDAG is likely the solution.
- **Simple Grouping:** If the goal is purely visual organization, Task Groups might be a lighter-weight alternative.
- **Shared Code:** For truly shared libraries of tasks, explore creating a full custom Airflow plugin.

Practical Exercise

1. **Break It Down:** Examine your most complex DAG. Are there multi-task sections that could be refactored into a SubDAG?
2. **Think Ahead:** If you're starting a new DAG, could you design it from the start with logical SubDAGs in mind to improve its maintainability?

Additional Resources

- **Airflow Docs on SubDAGs:**
  https://airflow.apache.org/docs/apache-airflow/stable/concepts/subdags.html
- **Blog Post: Why Use SubDAGs?**
  https://medium.com/analytics-vidhya/apache-airflow-what-why-and-how-part-2-dags-and-sub-dags-4746c8734c43

Next Up: Let's explore how Task Groups bring a different layer of streamlining and clarity to your Airflow pipelines!

Task Grouping Unleashed: Optimizing Workflows with TaskGroups

1. The Evolution of Workflow Organization

Airflow gives you a toolset for managing complexity, and its organizational features have become more sophisticated over time:

- **Basic DAGs:** In the beginning, there were just DAGs and the tasks within them.
- **SubDAGs:** Reusable chunks of logic and parameterization. A powerful leap forward.
- **Task Groups:** Introduced for streamlining the UI and mental model, without changing execution behavior.

2. When to Reach for Task Groups

Scenarios where Task Groups shine:

- **Logical Segmentation:** Your DAG has clear phases (setup, core processing, reporting) that deserve visual emphasis in the UI.
- **UI Decluttering:** Collapse a group of tasks that are currently less important, letting you focus on a specific problem area.
- **Team Ownership:** Different teams working on a single large DAG can have their areas of responsibility delineated with Task Groups.
- **Hiding Complexity:** For new users exploring your DAGs, collapsed Task Groups make the overall structure less intimidating.

3. Defining Task Groups

Let's use the syntax to make things concrete:

```python
from airflow import DAG
from airflow.operators.python import PythonOperator
from airflow.utils.dates import days_ago

with DAG(
        dag_id='grouped_dag',
        schedule_interval="@daily",
        start_date=days_ago(1),
) as dag:

    with TaskGroup("data_extraction") as extraction_group:
```

```
        fetch_user_data =
PythonOperator(task_id='fetch_user_data', ...)
        fetch_sales_data =
PythonOperator(task_id='fetch_sales_data', ...)

    with TaskGroup("processing") as processing_group:
        clean_data = PythonOperator(task_id='clean_data', ...)
        calculate_metrics =
PythonOperator(task_id='calculate_metrics', ...)

    store_results = PythonOperator(task_id='store_results',
...)

    extraction_group >> processing_group >> store_results
```

Key Points

- `TaskGroup` acts like a context manager (the `with` statement).
- Groups are for visual/logical purposes, **not execution isolation.**
- Dependencies can cross group boundaries.

4. Task Groups in Action

The primary way you'll interact with Task Groups is in Airflow's UI:

- **Graph View:** Neatly collapsed boxes representing your groups. Expand them to reveal the contained tasks.
- **DAGs List:** Filter the list of DAGs to only show those containing a certain group prefix – focus your attention.

5. Considerations & Cautions

- **Not a Silver Bullet:** Deeply inefficient tasks won't be magically fixed by grouping them. Task-level optimization still matters!
- **SubDAGs Remain Relevant:** If you need to pass data into/out of a block of logic, or if you truly need execution isolation, SubDAGs are still the right tool.
- **Nesting:** Task Groups can be nested within each other for hierarchical structures.

Practical Exercise

1. **Group Therapy:** Take your most complex DAG and try to sketch out how you could refactor it to use Task Groups. Does it fundamentally improve readability?

2. **Hypothetical Growth:** Imagine your DAG will double in complexity over the next six months. Would preemptively adding Task Groups make that growth easier to manage?

Additional Resources

- **Airflow Docs on Task Groups**
  https://airflow.apache.org/docs/apache-airflow/stable/concepts/task-groups.html

Next Up: Let's explore scenarios where the lines blur between SubDAGs and Task Groups, and how to choose the right technique for your Airflow workflows!

Evolving Strategies: Transitioning from SubDAGs to TaskGroups

1. Why Consider the Shift?

While SubDAGs are powerful, there are cases where Task Groups offer advantages:

- **UI Focus:** If the primary goal is to declutter the Airflow Graph View and improve navigation of complex DAGs, Task Groups are a lighter-weight solution.
- **Team-Based Views:** Task Groups can visually delineate areas of ownership within a DAG, which SubDAGs cannot do as directly.
- **Migrating Legacy DAGs:** If you have a very old DAG with no use of SubDAGs, adding Task Groups can be an incremental way to gain some organizational benefits without a full rewrite.

2. When SubDAGs Remain Essential

It's crucial to realize this isn't a one-size-fits-all replacement. SubDAGs are still the go-to for:

- **Parameterization:** When you need to pass distinct data into or out of a chunk of your workflow, SubDAGs are necessary.
- **Execution Isolation:** If a set of tasks needs its own retry logic, timeout settings, or should be insulated from failures in other parts of the DAG, SubDAGs provide this control.
- **Dynamic DAGs:** Task Groups are defined statically in your DAG code. SubDAGs can be generated on the fly, which is essential for some data-driven pipeline patterns.

3. The Transition Process

Let's assume you've identified a SubDAG that is a prime candidate for becoming a Task Group. Here's the general process:

1. **Dependency Mapping:** Carefully examine how tasks outside the SubDAG depend on tasks within it, and vice-versa. These dependencies will need to be adjusted.
2. **Refactoring:**
   - Delete the `SubDagOperator` that invoked the SubDAG.
   - Replace the SubDAG file with normal task definitions.
   - Enclose those tasks within a `TaskGroup` context manager.
   - Fix dependencies to point to the now directly included tasks.

3. **Testing (Meticulously!)** Because you're altering the dependency structure, rigorous testing is essential to ensure your logic hasn't changed unexpectedly.

4. Example: Simplified Reporting

Let's say your SubDAG (`reporting_subdag.py`) handles generating reports:

```python
# reporting_subdag.py
from airflow.operators.python import PythonOperator

def generate_sales_report(**context): ...

def generate_customer_report(**context): ...

# ... other report generation tasks
```

And is invoked in your main DAG like this:

```python
from airflow import DAG
from airflow.operators.subdag import SubDagOperator

reporting_subdag = SubDagOperator(
    task_id='reporting',
    subdag=create_reporting_subdag('main_dag.reporting'),
    dag=dag
)
```

After Transition:

```python
from airflow import DAG
from airflow.operators.python import PythonOperator

with TaskGroup(group_id='reporting') as reporting_group:
    generate_sales_report = PythonOperator(task_id='generate_sales_report', ...)
    generate_customer_report = PythonOperator(task_id='generate_customer_report', ...)

    # ... other report generation tasks
```

5. Considerations

- **Hybrids Are OK:** A single DAG can use both SubDAGs and Task Groups. Choose the right tool for each area of your workflow.
- **Version Control:** If refactoring a substantial DAG, use version control to track changes and have a rollback path if needed.

Practical Exercise

1. **SubDAG Audit:** Do you have SubDAGs that are simple enough in structure that they would be equally well represented by a Task Group?
2. **Hypothetical Impact:** If you converted a SubDAG to a Task Group, how would it change how you interact with that DAG within the Airflow UI?

Additional Resources

- **Airflow Blog on Task Groups:** https://airflow.apache.org/docs/apache-airflow/stable/concepts/task-groups.html

Task Collaboration: Maximizing Efficiency with TaskGroups

In previous chapters, we discussed optimizing DAG structures and explored the now-deprecated SubDAG concept. This chapter introduces the cornerstone of modular and efficient workflow design in modern Apache Airflow: TaskGroups. TaskGroups provide a powerful way to encapsulate related tasks, establishing a clear hierarchy within your data pipelines.

Why TaskGroups Matter

As the complexity of your data pipelines grows, these benefits of TaskGroups become paramount:

- **Organization and Readability:** TaskGroups compartmentalize logical sections of your DAGs, significantly improving their readability and maintainability. They effectively declutter the Airflow UI.
- **Encapsulation and Reusability:** TaskGroups promote the creation of reusable workflow components that you can easily plug into different pipelines. Imagine them as self-contained mini-DAGs.
- **Improved Error Handling:** If a task within a TaskGroup fails, you have granular control over how to handle the failure for the entire group.
- **Visual Clarity:** The Airflow UI neatly represents TaskGroups as collapsible units, providing a clearer visual overview of complex DAGs.

Introducing TaskGroups

Let's illustrate the core concept with a simple example. Suppose you have a DAG responsible for the following ETL tasks:

1. Extract data from a source.
2. Transform and cleanse the data.
3. Load it into your data warehouse.

Traditional Airflow Approach

```
from airflow import DAG
from airflow.operators.python import PythonOperator
from airflow.utils.dates import days_ago

with DAG(
    dag_id="etl_pipeline",
    default_args=default_args,
    start_date=days_ago(1),
```

```python
    schedule_interval="@daily"
) as dag:

    def extract_data():
        # ... logic to extract data

    def transform_data():
        # ... logic to transform data

    def load_data():
        # ... logic to load data

    extract_task = PythonOperator(task_id="extract", python_callable=extract_data)
    transform_task = PythonOperator(task_id="transform", python_callable=transform_data)
    load_task = PythonOperator(task_id="load", python_callable=load_data)

    extract_task >> transform_task >> load_task
```

TaskGroup Approach

```python
from airflow import DAG
from airflow.utils.task_group import TaskGroup
from airflow.operators.python import PythonOperator
from airflow.utils.dates import days_ago

with DAG(
    dag_id="etl_pipeline_with_taskgroups",
    default_args=default_args,
    start_date=days_ago(1),
    schedule_interval="@daily"
) as dag:

    with TaskGroup("data_processing") as processing_group:

        def extract_data():
            # ... logic to extract data

        def transform_data():
            # ... logic to transform data
```

```
    extract_task = PythonOperator(task_id="extract",
python_callable=extract_data)
    transform_task = PythonOperator(task_id="transform",
python_callable=transform_data)

    extract_task >> transform_task

  def load_data():
      # ... logic to load data

  load_task = PythonOperator(task_id="load",
python_callable=load_data)

  processing_group >> load_task
```

Notice how the TaskGroup encapsulates extraction and transformation, creating a logical unit within your DAG.

Nesting TaskGroups and Advanced Use Cases

TaskGroups support nesting for hierarchical workflow organization. Consider a more complex scenario, such as onboarding customers. You might structure it like this:

```
with TaskGroup("onboarding") as onboarding_group:
    with TaskGroup("customer_data_management") as
data_management:
        # Tasks for customer data handling ...
    with TaskGroup("subscriptions") as subscriptions:
        # Tasks for managing subscriptions ...
```

Moving Beyond SubDAGs (With Caution)

While TaskGroups are the preferred tool, it's crucial to note that SubDAGs are still available, though deprecated. Use them sparingly for legacy use cases or specific migration needs.

Additional Resources

- **Airflow Documentation: TaskGroups**
  https://airflow.apache.org/docs/apache-airflow/stable/concepts/task-groups.html

Embracing Data Exchange: Adding XCom Functionality

In complex data pipelines, it's often necessary for tasks to communicate and share data seamlessly. Airflow's XCom functionality provides a robust mechanism for passing information between tasks, enabling powerful workflow orchestration.

Understanding XComs

- **The Core Concept:** XComs (cross-communication) are a key-value store system intrinsic to Airflow. Tasks can 'push' (write) data as XCom values, and subsequent tasks can 'pull' (read) those values, creating a channel for data exchange within a DAG.
- **Behind the Scenes:** Airflow leverages its metadata database to store and retrieve XCom data efficiently.

Key Use Cases

1. **Data Transfer:** Passing small-to-medium sized data between tasks like extracted information, status codes, file paths, transformed data, or calculated metrics.
2. **Coordination and Signaling:** Communicating decision points or outcomes from one task to another, influencing downstream dependencies.
3. **Sharing Intermediate Results:** Persisting data during a DAG's execution for later access or analysis, making data pipelines more versatile.

XComs in Action

Let's illustrate with an example. Suppose you have a DAG:

1. **Task A:** Extracts data from a source API.
2. **Task B:** Transforms the raw data
3. **Task C:** Loads the data into a data warehouse

Traditional Approach (no XComs): Tasks A, B, C would have to independently establish connections, potentially duplicating effort and increasing the potential for inconsistencies.

XCom Approach:

```
from airflow import DAG
from airflow.operators.python import PythonOperator
from airflow.utils.dates import days_ago
```

```
with DAG(
    dag_id="xcom_dag",
    default_args=default_args,
    start_date=days_ago(1),
    schedule_interval="@daily"
) as dag:

    def extract_data():
        data = # ... extract from a source API
        return data

    def transform_data(ti):
        raw_data = ti.xcom_pull(task_ids='extract_data')
        transformed_data = # ... transformation logic
        return transformed_data

    def load_data(ti):
        final_data = ti.xcom_pull(task_ids='transform_data')
        # ... load data to the warehouse

    extract_task = PythonOperator(task_id="extract_data",
python_callable=extract_data)
    transform_task = PythonOperator(task_id="transform_data",
python_callable=transform_data)
    load_task = PythonOperator(task_id="load_data",
python_callable=load_data)

    extract_task >> transform_task >> load_task
```

In this setup:

- `extract_data` pushes the extracted data to XComs.
- `transform_data` pulls from XComs using `ti.xcom_pull()`, receiving the data produced by `extract_data`.
- `load_data` repeats the pattern, using the transformed output.

Best Practices and Considerations

- **Data Size:** XComs are ideal for smaller datasets. For large data, use an external storage system (database, object store) and pass references via XComs.

- **Clearing XCom Values:** Clear XComs regularly to avoid database bloat, especially within frequently running DAGs. Use the `clear=True` parameter in your tasks. ([invalid URL removed])
- **Return Values vs. XCom:** Return values from PythonOperators are automatically pushed into XComs, providing a convenient shortcut.

Additional Resources

- **Airflow Documentation: XComs**
  https://airflow.apache.org/docs/apache-airflow/stable/concepts/xcoms.html

Important Note: Remember to emphasize the preference of TaskGroups for modularity when building new pipelines, while acknowledging the continued availability of XComs.

Data Dialogue: Facilitating Task Communication with XComs

In the previous chapter, we discussed encapsulating workflows within SubDAGs. This chapter explores XComs, Airflow's native mechanism for inter-task communication, allowing tasks to share data and orchestrate complex dependencies.

XComs: The Heart of Task Collaboration

At their core, XComs provide a way to pass messages between tasks within a DAG. Imagine them as a communication channel built into your pipelines:

- **Pushing Data:** When a task completes, it can 'push' information to XComs. This information is stored under a unique key.
- **Pulling Data:** Subsequent tasks can 'pull' values from XComs by referencing the key.

Practical Example: ETL Workflow Coordination

Let's revisit the classic Extract, Transform, Load (ETL) process:

1. **Extract (`extract_data`):** Fetches raw data from a database, API, or file.
2. **Transform (`transform_data`):** Cleans, processes, and normalizes the data for analysis.
3. **Load (`load_data`):** Writes the final data to a data warehouse or reporting system.

Using XComs:

- `extract_data` might push the number of records extracted.
- `transform_data` could pull this record count and include it in a quality control metric, logging both input and output record numbers.
- `load_data` could pull status updates from previous tasks to provide feedback in monitoring tools or alerts.

Code Illustration

```python
from airflow import DAG
from airflow.operators.python import PythonOperator
from airflow.utils.dates import days_ago

with DAG(
    dag_id="etl_xcoms",
```

```python
    default_args=default_args,
    start_date=days_ago(1),
    schedule_interval="@daily"
) as dag:

    def extract_data():
        # ... logic to fetch data
        num_records = len(data)
        return num_records

    def transform_data(ti):
        input_records = ti.xcom_pull(task_ids='extract_data')
        # ... transformation logic
        return transformed_data

    def load_data(ti):
        final_data = ti.xcom_pull(task_ids='transform_data')
        # ... data loading process

    extract_task = PythonOperator(task_id="extract_data",
python_callable=extract_data)
    transform_task = PythonOperator(task_id="transform_data",
python_callable=transform_data)
    load_task = PythonOperator(task_id="load_data",
python_callable=load_data)

    extract_task >> transform_task >> load_task
```

XComs Beyond Data Transfer

XComs can exchange more than just data. Consider these use cases:

- **Sharing Metadata:** Pass timestamps, source/target system IDs, or job run IDs.
- **Signaling:** Task A sets a flag in XComs, triggering downstream processes in Task B.
- **Conditional Branching:** Task A's output dictates which task (B or C) executes next (See Chapter 77 for more on conditional logic).

Best Practices and Reminders

- **Judicious Use:** While powerful, excessive XCom usage can impact database performance. For large data, store it in a database or object store, passing references via XComs.

- **Return Values:** Returning a value from a PythonOperator automatically pushes it into XComs, offering a convenient shortcut.
- **Templating:** Leverage Jinja templating within XCom values for dynamic exchanges.

Additional Resources

- **Airflow Documentation: XComs**
  https://airflow.apache.org/docs/apache-airflow/stable/concepts/xcoms.html

Remember: TaskGroups are generally the preferred approach for modularization, and XComs serve as the communication fabric within and between complex data pipelines.

XComs in Motion: Witnessing Data Sharing in Action

In the previous chapter, we discussed XComs as the key communication mechanism within Airflow DAGs. Now, let's see XComs in practice, demonstrating how they enable seamless data flow and coordination in complex data pipelines.

Illustrative Examples

We'll focus on three scenarios that highlight common and powerful XCom use cases:

- **Example 1: ETL Coordination**
  An ETL pipeline where:
  - **Extract Task** fetches raw data from a database, API, or file.
  - **Transform Task** cleanses and restructures the data.
  - **Load Task** loads the transformed data into the final destination.
  - **XCom Usage:**
    - Extract Task pushes the record count.
    - Transform Task pulls the count, logs input/output records for quality checks.
    - Load Task pulls status flags from prior tasks, sending an alert if any step failed.
- **Example 2: Parameter Passing**
  A pipeline with dependent dynamic tasks:
  - **Config Task:** Reads a config file determining the countries to process.
  - **Data Fetch Tasks (Dynamic):** One task spawned per country, fetching relevant data.
  - **Aggregation Task:** Aggregates all country-specific datasets.
  - **XCom Usage:**
    - Config Task pushes the country list.
    - Each Data Fetch Task pulls the countries it should process.
    - Aggregation Task pulls processing status from each Data Fetch Task to ensure completion.
- **Example 3: Conditional Branching**
  - **Validation Task:** Checks data quality.
  - **Process High-Quality Task**
  - **Process Low-Quality Task**
  - **XCom Usage:**
    - Validation Task pushes a quality flag (`high/low`).
    - XCom determines path execution: high-quality data vs. additional fixes applied by the low-quality process task.

Code Snippet (Example 1)

```python
from airflow import DAG
from airflow.operators.python import PythonOperator
from airflow.utils.dates import days_ago

with DAG(
    dag_id="xcom_etl_example",
    default_args=default_args,
    start_date=days_ago(1),
    schedule_interval="@daily"
) as dag:

    def extract_data():
        # ... data extraction logic
        return num_records

    def transform_data(ti):
        input_records = ti.xcom_pull(task_ids='extract_data')
        # ... transformation logic
        return transformed_data

    def load_data(ti):
        status = ti.xcom_pull(task_ids=['extract_data', 'transform_data'])
        # ... loading logic, potentially using status flags

    extract_task = PythonOperator(task_id="extract_data", python_callable=extract_data)
    transform_task = PythonOperator(task_id="transform_data", python_callable=transform_data)
    load_task = PythonOperator(task_id="load_data", python_callable=load_data)

    extract_task >> transform_task >> load_task
```

Visualizing XComs in the Airflow UI

1. **Graph View:** Hovering over tasks shows the option "XComs" which displays values passed.
2. **XCom Tab:** Provides a dedicated view of all XComs, including keys, values, timestamps, and originating tasks.

Key Points and Considerations

- **Alternatives for Larger Data:** When dealing with large amounts of data, pass file paths or database references via XComs, not the raw data itself.
- **Best Practices:** Clear naming conventions and documentation make XCom exchanges more understandable.

Additional Resources

- **Airflow Docs: XComs**
  https://airflow.apache.org/docs/apache-airflow/stable/concepts/xcoms.html

Directing the Flow: Navigating Conditional Path Execution

Airflow DAGs often resemble decision trees, where workflows branch based on data, external conditions, or even success/failure of previous tasks. This chapter teaches you how to orchestrate those decision points, making your pipelines dynamic and responsive.

The Core Concept: Conditional Branching

At its heart, conditional path execution is about asking questions within your DAG and letting the answers determine the path taken:

- **Did a data quality check pass?** If yes, proceed to analysis; if not, trigger remediation tasks.
- **Is new data available in a source system?** If yes, start processing; if not, wait or gracefully handle the no-data scenario.
- **Did a critical upstream process complete successfully?** If no, send alerts before dependent tasks fail.

Key Mechanisms

Airflow offers tools to implement this logic:

- **BranchPythonOperator:** A special operator that evaluates a Python function to decide which branch to follow.
- **Task Trigger Rules:** Fine-grained control over how a task's completion (or failure) influences downstream tasks.
- **XComs:** When combined with conditional operators, XComs provide decision-making based on data produced by previous tasks.

Example: Data Validation with Branching

Imagine a DAG with these tasks:

1. **Fetch Data**
2. **Validate Data**
3. **Process Valid Data**
4. **Remediate Invalid Data**

Code Implementation (BranchPythonOperator Example)

```
from airflow import DAG
from airflow.operators.python import PythonOperator, BranchPythonOperator
```

```python
from airflow.utils.dates import days_ago

with DAG(
    dag_id="conditional_dag",
    default_args=default_args,
    start_date=days_ago(1),
    schedule_interval="@daily"
) as dag:

    def fetch_data():
        # ... fetch data
        return data

    def is_data_valid(data):
        # ... validation logic
        return data_is_valid

    def process_data(data):
        # ... process valid data

    def remediate_data(data):
        # ... handle invalid data

    fetch_task = PythonOperator(task_id="fetch_data", python_callable=fetch_data)
    validate_task = PythonOperator(task_id="validate_data", python_callable=is_data_valid)
    branch_task = BranchPythonOperator(task_id="branch", python_callable=is_data_valid)
    process_task = PythonOperator(task_id="process_data", python_callable=process_data)
    remediate_task = PythonOperator(task_id="remediate_data", python_callable=remediate_data)

    fetch_task >> validate_task >> branch_task
    branch_task >> process_task
    branch_task >> remediate_task
```

Trigger Rules in Action

Let's say you only want `process_data` to run if `validate_data` was successful. Trigger rules refine the dependency between them:

```
validate_task >> branch_task >> process_task
[trigger_rule="all_success"]
```

Tips and Considerations

- **Clear Logic:** Keep your conditional functions and trigger rules well-documented for maintainability.
- **XCom Enhancement:** Use XComs to pass data used in decision-making between tasks.
- **Modularization:** Consider TaskGroups for encapsulating branches, especially if logic grows complex.

Additional Resources

- **Airflow Documentation: Branching**
  https://airflow.apache.org/docs/apache-airflow/stable/concepts/branching.html
- **Airflow Documentation: Trigger Rules**
  https://airflow.apache.org/docs/apache-airflow/stable/concepts/trigger-rules.html

Conditional Execution: Executing Tasks Based on Conditions

In the previous chapter, we discussed directing workflow logic using conditional branching. This chapter delves deeper into customizing task execution based on various criteria, making your DAGs responsive to their environment.

Key Scenarios

Here's when conditional execution is essential:

- **Data-Driven Decisions:**
    - Execute processing steps only if new data is available.
    - Trigger different actions based on the quality or content of the data.
- **External Dependencies:**
    - Run tasks only after upstream systems have completed their processes.
    - Send alerts if external services are unavailable.
- **Error Handling and Adaptability:**
    - Implement different retry or remediation paths depending on the type of failure encountered.

Mechanisms for Conditional Execution

Airflow provides several tools working together to achieve this flexibility:

1. **BranchPythonOperator:** This core operator evaluates a Python function that returns the task_id of the next task to execute. (See the previous chapter, "Directing the Flow," for an in-depth discussion).
2. **Short-Circuiting:** Control the execution of an entire branch based on an initial task's state. A simple example:

```
check_data >> task_a >> task_b   [trigger_rule="all_success"]
check_data >> task_c             [trigger_rule="all_failed"]
```

- If check_data succeeds, only task_a and task_b run.
- If check_data fails, only task_c runs.

2. **XComs:** Use data pulled from XComs as the decision point. For example, a task could set a status flag that subsequent tasks use to determine their execution path.
3. **External Task Sensors:** Defer execution of tasks until a signal is received from a system outside your DAG,

Illustrative Example: Quality-Driven Processing

Let's modify our ETL:

1. **Data Quality Check:** Evaluates data metrics (completeness, validity, etc.).
2. **Process High-Quality:** Perform in-depth analysis and modeling.
3. **Remediate Low-Quality:** Apply fixes and reprocessing.
4. **Alert Task:** Send detailed notifications, especially for low-quality scenarios.

Code Snippet

```python
from airflow import DAG
from airflow.operators.python import PythonOperator, BranchPythonOperator
from airflow.operators.bash import BashOperator
from airflow.utils.dates import days_ago

with DAG(
    dag_id="conditional_etl",
    default_args=default_args,
    start_date=days_ago(1),
    schedule_interval="@daily"
) as dag:

    def check_quality(ti):
        data_quality = ti.xcom_pull(task_ids='extract_data')
        return 'process_data' if data_quality['score'] > 0.8 else 'remediate_data'

    extract_task = PythonOperator(task_id="extract_data", python_callable=extract_data)

    check_task = PythonOperator(task_id="check_quality", python_callable=check_quality)

    branch_task = BranchPythonOperator(task_id="branch", python_callable=check_quality)

    process_task = BashOperator(task_id="process_data", bash_command="...")

    remediate_task = BashOperator(task_id="remediate_data", bash_command="...")

    alert_task = PythonOperator(task_id="alert", python_callable=send_alert)
```

```
extract_task >> check_task >> branch_task
branch_task >> process_task >> alert_task
branch_task >> remediate_task >> alert_task
```

Best Practices

- **Clarity:** Document the logic behind conditional execution carefully for maintainability.
- **Encapsulation:** TaskGroups excel at grouping tasks within conditional branches.

Additional Resources

- **Airflow Docs: Branching**
  https://airflow.apache.org/docs/apache-airflow/stable/concepts/branching.html
- **Airflow Docs: Short-Circuiting**
  https://airflow.apache.org/docs/apache-airflow/stable/concepts/short-circuiting.html
- **Blog: Conditional Logic Examples**
  https://www.datasciencecentral.com/profiles/blogs/conditional-logic-examples

Triggering Transformation: Understanding Task Trigger Rules

In previous chapters, we've explored how to control the path of execution; now, let's add another dimension – fine-grained control over when tasks actually run. Task Trigger Rules refine dependencies within your DAGs for intelligent automation.

The Power of Trigger Rules

At their core, trigger rules answer the question: "Under what circumstances should a task execute based on the outcome of its upstream tasks?"

They offer these key advantages:

- **Granular Control:** Move beyond simple success/fail dependencies. React to different failure modes, skipped tasks, or even specific conditions met by upstream tasks.
- **Workflow Responsiveness:** No more waiting for tasks that aren't necessary. React dynamically to data or external conditions as reflected by upstream tasks.
- **Reduced Resource Waste:** Avoid executing unnecessary steps, conserving computational resources, and potentially saving costs.

Trigger Rules in Action

Let's look at common trigger rules and when you'd use them:

- `all_success` (Default): Task runs if *all* upstream tasks succeeded.
- `all_failed`: Task runs if *all* upstream tasks failed. Useful for consolidated error handling or cleanup.
- `all_done`: Task runs regardless of upstream states; use for finalization actions.
- `one_failed`: Task runs if *at least* one upstream task failed.
- `one_success`: Task runs if *at least* one upstream task succeeded.
- `none_failed`: Task runs if *none* of the upstream tasks failed (but some might be skipped).
- `none_skipped`: Task runs if *no* upstream task was skipped; ensures all required upstream processes happened.
- `dummy`: Task is always triggered, useful for workflow orchestration without being dependent on previous task states.

Example: ETL with Trigger Rules

1. **Extract Data**
2. **Validate Data Quality**
    - `all_success`: -> Process High-Quality Data
    - `one_failed`: -> Process Low-Quality Data
    - `all_done`: -> Send Alert

Code Illustration

```python
from airflow import DAG
from airflow.operators.python import PythonOperator
from airflow.utils.dates import days_ago

with DAG(
    dag_id="etl_with_trigger_rules",
    default_args=default_args,
    start_date=days_ago(1),
    schedule_interval="@daily"
) as dag:

    # ... tasks definitions for extract, validate, process_hq, process_lq, alert

    extract >> validate
    validate >> process_hq [trigger_rule="all_success"]
    validate >> process_lq [trigger_rule="one_failed"]
    validate >> alert      [trigger_rule="all_done"]
```

Best Practices and Considerations

- **Complexity vs. TaskGroups:** For simpler logic, trigger rules are excellent. For complex scenarios encapsulate branches within TaskGroups.
- **Clarity:** Document the reasoning behind your trigger rule choices.
- **Cross-DAG Dependencies:** If you need to react to the state of another DAG, consider using ExternalTaskSensor or dataset concepts (Chapter 51).

Advanced Techniques

Trigger Rules can even be customized, but this is a very advanced use case often signaling a design pattern that could be better represented with TaskGroups.

Additional Resources

- **Airflow Documentation: Trigger Rules**
  https://airflow.apache.org/docs/apache-airflow/stable/concepts/operators.html#trigger-rules

Rule Refinement: Enhancing BranchPythonOperator with Trigger Rules

We've harnessed the power of `BranchPythonOperator` for conditional branching and trigger rules for fine-grained task execution control. Now, let's explore a power user technique: customizing how the `BranchPythonOperator` itself reacts to upstream tasks.

The Challenge

By default, `BranchPythonOperator` behaves like any other task when it comes to trigger rules:

- It runs if its upstream tasks succeed (`all_success`).
- It doesn't run if upstream tasks fail (`all_failed`).

But what if you want the branching decision-making task to *always* run, even if upstream processes failed, so you can dynamically handle failures within your workflow logic?

Custom Trigger Rules to the Rescue

Airflow allows defining custom trigger rules. Here's the strategy:

1. **Create a Custom Rule:** Write a Python function that takes an instance of `TaskInstance` and returns the desired trigger state (e.g., always 'success').
2. **Integrate into `BranchPythonOperator`:** Pass your custom rule's name to the `trigger_rule` parameter of your `BranchPythonOperator`.

Illustrative Example

Let's say you want a branch decision task to always execute to determine remediation steps after a validation step, regardless of the validation outcome:

```
from airflow import DAG
from airflow.operators.python import PythonOperator, BranchPythonOperator
 from airflow.utils.dates import days_ago
from airflow.utils.trigger_rule import TriggerRule

def always_run_branching(**kwargs):
```

```python
    # Your logic to determine which branch to take
    return "remediate_data"

def custom_trigger_rule(task_instance):
    """ Trigger this task always, regardless of upstream state"""
    return TriggerRule.ALWAYS

with DAG(
    dag_id="branching_refinement",
    default_args=default_args,
    start_date=days_ago(1),
    schedule_interval="@daily"
) as dag:

    validate_data = PythonOperator(task_id="validate_data", python_callable=...)

    branch_decision = BranchPythonOperator(
        task_id="branch_decision",
        python_callable=always_run_branching,
        trigger_rule=custom_trigger_rule
    )

    remediate_data = PythonOperator(task_id="remediate_data", python_callable=...)

    validate_data >> branch_decision >> remediate_data
```

Key Considerations

- **Use Judiciously:** This is a powerful but advanced pattern. Overuse can make DAGs harder to reason about. If upstream task health matters to the branching condition itself, consider XComs or TaskGroups.
- **Debugging:** Carefully test your custom logic, as trigger rule behavior can be complex.

Why Do This?

- **Centralized Error Handling:** React to diverse upstream failure modes within the branching logic.

- **Dynamic Workflow Adaptation:** The `BranchPythonOperator` always executes, enabling on-the-fly adjustments to downstream steps based on the state of the pipeline

Additional Notes

- Airflow provides several built-in trigger rules like `TriggerRule.ONE_SUCCESS`, `TriggerRule.ONE_FAILED`, etc. Explore these before writing fully custom rules.
- **Airflow Evolution:** Custom trigger rules are still supported but less necessary as TaskGroups become the preferred way to encapsulate complex logic with their robust dependency management features.

Section 8:
Crafting Airflow Plugins with Elasticsearch and PostgreSQL

Prelude to Plugin Power: Introduction to Airflow Plugin Development

In previous chapters, we leveraged the built-in Operators, Sensors, and Hooks that form the backbone of Airflow. Now, unlock a new level of customization: build your own components to integrate with the unique tools and systems within your data ecosystem.

Why Build Plugins?

- **Tailored Solutions:** Craft Operators, Hooks, and more that interact seamlessly with your specific databases, internal APIs, or proprietary platforms.
- **Encapsulation:** Bundle reusable logic into well-defined plugins, promoting code maintainability and making your Airflow workflows cleaner.
- **Community Contributions:** Share your plugins with the wider Airflow community, helping solve common data engineering problems collaboratively.

The Essence of Airflow Plugins

At their core, Airflow plugins are simply Python packages following a specific structure. Within these packages, you'll extend Airflow's core classes to:

- **Create Custom Operators:** Define new types of tasks (e.g., `MyCustomDataTransferOperator`).
- **Implement New Hooks:** Provide interfaces to external systems (e.g., `MyCompanyMetricsHook`).
- **Add Executors:** Introduce new task execution strategies (though this is less common)
- **Extend the UI:** Include custom views and visualizations within the Airflow web interface (a very advanced use case).

Key Concepts (The Building Blocks)

1. **Airflow Base Classes:** You'll inherit from classes like `BaseOperator`, `BaseSensorOperator`, and `BaseHook` to provide the framework for your components.
2. **Discoverability:** Airflow has a designated `plugins` folder. Placing your packages here makes them discoverable by the Airflow environment.
3. **Metadata:** Your plugin components will define attributes to help Airflow understand how to use them.

A Simple Example (Hypothetical)

Let's imagine a plugin for a company's internal task management system:

```python
from airflow.plugins_manager import AirflowPlugin
from airflow.models import BaseOperator

class MyCompanyTaskOperator(BaseOperator):
    def __init__(self, task_name, *args, **kwargs):
        super().__init__(**kwargs)
        self.task_name = task_name

    def execute(self, context):
        # Logic to interact with company's task system,
        # update task status, etc.

class MyCompanyPlugin(AirflowPlugin):
    name = "mycompany_plugin"
    operators = [MyCompanyTaskOperator]
```

Before You Start Coding

- **Solid Airflow Fundamentals:** Comfort with DAGs, Operators, and the Airflow architecture is essential.
- **Environment Setup:** You'll need a development area to create and test your plugin packages.

What's Next?

In subsequent chapters, we'll dive into:

- **Elasticsearch Integration:** Building Operators and Hooks to work with Elasticsearch.
- **The Plugin Paradigm:** Understanding plugin structure in detail.
- **Hook Creation:** The heart of connecting to external systems.

Additional Resources

- **Airflow Documentation: Plugins**
  https://airflow.apache.org/docs/apache-airflow/stable/plugins/index.html
- **Example Plugin Repository:**
  https://github.com/apache/airflow/tree/main/airflow/plugins

Ready to Empower Your Workflows? Plugin development is like handing Airflow an advanced toolkit tailor-made for the challenges you face.

Exploring Elasticsearch: Unveiling its Significance in Data Management

Airflow excels at orchestrating data movement and transformations. To unleash the full potential of the data you've meticulously processed, you need a robust solution for storing, searching, and analyzing it. Enter Elasticsearch.

What is Elasticsearch?

At its core, Elasticsearch is a:

- **Distributed Search Engine:** It excels at blazing-fast full-text search across massive datasets. Think of it like a supercharged search bar for your structured and unstructured data.
- **Document Store:** Optimized for storing semi-structured data in JSON format.
- **Analytics Platform:** It includes built-in aggregations, visualizations (Kibana), and machine learning capabilities, enabling you to extract insights from your data.

Why Elasticsearch + Airflow?

1. **Log Analysis:** Airflow generates detailed logs. Pipe them into Elasticsearch for search, monitoring, and alerting based on log patterns.
2. **Metrics Storage:** Stream operational metrics from your data pipeline into Elasticsearch for real-time dashboards and visualizations.
3. **Search-Driven Applications:** An Airflow DAG could process data, load it into Elasticsearch, and power an application's search functionality, providing users with fast, relevant search results.
4. **Anomaly Detection:** With Elasticsearch's machine learning capabilities, analyze data indexed from your Airflow workflows to identify unusual patterns potentially signaling errors or unexpected changes in data quality.

Elasticsearch Essentials

Let's introduce some key terms for working with Elasticsearch:

- **Index:** Like a database in the relational world. An index houses related documents.
- **Document:** A JSON object containing your data. A single document could represent a log entry, a product, or a user profile.
- **Field:** A key-value pair within a document.
- **Mapping:** Defines the structure of documents in an index (similar to a table schema): field names and data types.

- **Inverted Index:** Elasticsearch's secret weapon for lightning-fast searches. It maps keywords to the documents they appear in, allowing for quick retrieval.

Example Scenario: Analyzing Website Traffic

Imagine you have an Airflow DAG:

1. **Extracts web server logs**
2. **Transforms logs into structured JSON**
3. **Loads logs into an Elasticsearch index**

With Elasticsearch, you could:

- **Search:** Find error logs matching specific criteria or user sessions based on IP address.
- **Visualize:** Build Kibana dashboards tracking traffic trends, error rates, etc.
- **Alerts:** Configure Elasticsearch to trigger actions when unusual activity is detected (e.g., sudden spike in 500 errors).

Preparing for Integration

Before integrating with Airflow, you'll need:

1. **Elasticsearch Cluster:**** A running Elasticsearch setup (locally, self-managed, or via cloud provider).
2. **Client Libraries:** Use Elasticsearch's Python client to interact with your cluster from Airflow.

What's Next?

In upcoming chapters, we'll cover:

- **Integration with Airflow:** Configuring Airflow to connect to Elasticsearch.
- **ElasticHook:** Creating an Airflow Hook for simplified Elasticsearch interactions within DAGs.
- **Best Practices:** Optimizing Elasticsearch usage for Airflow workloads.

Additional Resources

- **Elasticsearch Documentation:** https://www.elastic.co/guide/en/elasticsearch/reference/current/index.html
- **Elasticsearch for Log Analysis:** https://www.elastic.co/solutions/logging
- **Kibana Website:** https://www.elastic.co/kibana

Airflow and Elasticsearch Integration: Configuring Elasticsearch for Airflow

In the previous chapter, we discussed the powerful reasons to integrate Elasticsearch with Airflow. Now, let's get practical and ensure your Elasticsearch setup is primed to play nicely with your data pipelines.

Prerequisites

- **Elasticsearch Up and Running:** You have an Elasticsearch cluster deployed and accessible – locally, on a server, or via a managed service provider.
- **Network Accessibility:** Confirm that your Airflow environment can reach your Elasticsearch cluster over the network (consider firewalls, etc.).

Key Configuration Areas

1. **Elasticsearch Cluster Connection**
   - **Hostname/IP:** The address where Airflow can find your Elasticsearch cluster.
   - **Port:** The port Elasticsearch usually listens on (default: 9200).
   - **Authentication:** If security is enabled, provide username and password.
   - **Scheme:** Specify 'http' or 'https' as needed.
2. **Index Naming**
   - **Patterns:** Decide if DAGs should use default index names or if you'll customize index creation with patterns (e.g., `my_dag_run_{{ ds }}`)
   - **Time-Based Indices:** Consider if data should be stored in daily, weekly, or monthly indices for easier management.
3. **Mapping Considerations (Optional)**
   - If you have strong expectations about your data's structure, you can predefine field mappings in Elasticsearch. Most commonly, Airflow will infer these from your data.

Where to Configure: Airflow Connections

Airflow has a dedicated Connections UI, making setup and management streamlined.

- **Connection Id:** Give your connection a descriptive name (e.g., `elasticsearch_default`).
- **Connection Type:** Select 'Elasticsearch'.
- **Fields:** Enter the hostname, port, authentication details, and any index naming preferences as discussed above.

Example Configuration

A simple example in the Connections UI might look like this:

- Conn Id: `elasticsearch_default`
- Conn Type: Elasticsearch
- Host: `https://my-elasticsearch.com`
- Port: `9200`
- Login: `airflow_user`
- Password: `<your_password>`

Advanced Settings (Less Common)

The Connections UI exposes additional options:

- **Verify SSL:** Enforce certificate validation if using HTTPS.
- **Custom Certificates:** Use if you have self-signed certificates.

Beyond the Basics

- **Multiple Clusters:** Airflow supports defining multiple Elasticsearch connections to target different clusters if your use cases demand it.
- **Security Best Practices:** Always protect your Elasticsearch cluster with appropriate authentication and network security measures. Rotate credentials as needed.

Testing Your Connection

Once you've saved your connection:

1. **Airflow UI:** The connections list should show it as active.
2. **Test Code:** Write a simple PythonOperator that uses the Elasticsearch Python client to try indexing a test document.

Troubleshooting

- **Airflow Logs:** Check the Airflow logs if you encounter issues.
- **Elasticsearch Logs:** Inspect your Elasticsearch logs for connection attempts and errors.
- **Network Tools:** Use basic network tools (`ping`, `telnet`) to test connectivity between Airflow and Elasticsearch.

Additional Resources

- **Airflow Documentation: Elasticsearch Connection**
  https://airflow.apache.org/docs/apache-airflow-providers-elasticsearch/stable/operators/elasticsearch.html
- **Elasticsearch Python Client Guide**
  https://elasticsearch-py.readthedocs.io/en/latest/

Unveiling the Plugin Paradigm: Understanding the Plugin Architecture

In the world of Airflow, plugins are your key to extending functionality. But just how do they work? Let's unveil the architectural principles behind them.

Components of a Plugin

Think of a plugin as a self-contained package with the following potential ingredients:

1. **Custom Operators:** New types of tasks to encapsulate interactions with your specific systems and tools (e.g., `MyCompanyDataTransferOperator`).
2. **Custom Hooks:** Interfaces to external systems. Ideal for reusing connections and logic across tasks (e.g., `MyCompanyMetricsHook`).
3. **Executors:** If you were to define entirely new ways of executing tasks (though this is less common).
4. **Sensors:** New ways to monitor the state of external systems before proceeding (e.g., `MyCompanyJobCompletionSensor`).
5. **UI/Views (Advanced):** Custom elements to add to the Airflow web interface.

It's All About Classes

At the heart of a plugin, you'll find Python classes. To make your components discoverable by Airflow, these classes must inherit from Airflow's base classes:

- **Operators:** Base class `BaseOperator`
- **Hooks:** Base class `BaseHook`
- **Executors:** Base class `BaseExecutor`
- **Sensors:** Base class `BaseSensorOperator`

The Magic of the Plugins Folder

Airflow has a designated `plugins` directory. Consider it the portal through which Airflow discovers your creations. Here's how the structure typically looks:

```
your_airflow_home/
  plugins/
    my_company_plugin/
      __init__.py
      operators/
        my_company_transfer_operator.py
      hooks/
        my_company_metrics_hook.py
```

Essential Metadata

Your plugin files will define attributes and methods to:

- **Declare Identity:** Your plugin classes need to give Airflow their names.
- **Provide Behavior:** Implement the core logic (e.g., the `execute()` method of an Operator actually does the work).

Example: Operator Structure

Let's simplify the `MyCompanyTaskOperator` from earlier:

```python
from airflow.plugins_manager import AirflowPlugin
from airflow.models import BaseOperator
from airflow.utils.decorators import apply_defaults

class MyCompanyTaskOperator(BaseOperator):

    @apply_defaults
    def __init__(self, my_task_parameter, *args, **kwargs):
        super().__init__(*args, **kwargs)
        self.my_task_parameter = my_task_parameter

    def execute(self, context):
        # Logic to perform the task using 'my_task_parameter'

class MyCompanyPlugin(AirflowPlugin):
    name = "my_company_plugin"
    operators = [MyCompanyTaskOperator]
```

Key Points

- **Discoverability:** Placing your package in the `plugins` folder is crucial.
- **Organization:** Structure your plugin with subfolders for operators, hooks, etc., to maintain clarity.
- **Framework Integration:** Inheriting from Airflow base classes provides the 'wiring' to integrate with Airflow.

How Airflow Finds Your Treasures

Airflow regularly scans the `plugins` folder. It uses a process called *dynamic reflection* to discover your plugin components based on the class inheritance structure.

What's Next?

Now that you understand the architecture, we're ready for hands-on action:

- **Connections:** We'll learn how to manage connection information for your custom Hooks.
- **The ElasticHook:** A practical deep dive into creating a Hook for interacting with Elasticsearch.

Additional Resources

- **Airflow Documentation: Plugins**
  https://airflow.apache.org/docs/apache-airflow/stable/plugins/index.html
- **Airflow Codebase (Great for Examples):** https://github.com/apache/airflow
  Explore the plugins that ship with Airflow on GitHub.

Establishing Connections: Configuring Connections for Elasticsearch

In the previous chapter, we discussed how to configure Elasticsearch itself. Now, let's teach Airflow how to speak Elasticsearch's language. This is where Airflow Connections come into play.

The Role of Airflow Connections

Connections in Airflow provide a centralized and reusable way to store authentication details, hostnames, ports – any information necessary to interact with external systems. This includes:

- **Databases**
- **Cloud services**
- **Message queues**
- **And of course, Elasticsearch**

Setting up an Elasticsearch Connection

Airflow gives you a couple of ways to manage Connections:

1. **Airflow UI:**
    - Navigate to **Admin -> Connections**.
    - Click **Add a new record** and choose 'Elasticsearch' as the Connection Type.
2. **Environment Variables:**
    - The variable name follows the format `AIRFLOW_CONN_{CONN_ID}`, with the Conn Id in uppercase (*important!*). The value is a URI (e.g., `AIRFLOW_CONN_ELASTICSEARCH_DEFAULT='elasticsearch://myuser:mypass@my-elasticsearch.com:9200'`)

Breaking Down the Connection Fields

- **Conn Id:** The unique reference name you'll use in your DAGs (e.g., `elasticsearch_default`).
- **Conn Type:** 'Elasticsearch'.
- **Host:** Address of your Elasticsearch server (could be an IP or a domain like `my-elasticsearch.com`).
- **Port:** Typically 9200, but adjust if your Elasticsearch setup is different.
- **Schema:** `http` or `https` depending on your security setup.
- **Login:** Username if authentication is enabled.
- **Password:** The associated password.

Example UI Configuration

Let's say your Elasticsearch is at `https://my-elasticsearch.net` with the username `airflow` and password `securepassword`:

- **Conn Id:** elasticsearch_default
- **Conn Type:** Elasticsearch
- **Host:** my-elasticsearch.net
- **Port:** 443 (HTTPS default port)
- **Schema:** https
- **Login:** airflow
- **Password:** securepassword

Security Best Practices

- **HTTPS: Strongly** consider enforcing HTTPS for your Elasticsearch connections in production environments!
- **Secrets Management:** Explore secrets management tools (like Vault or your cloud provider's secrets service) rather than storing Elasticsearch credentials directly in the Airflow UI or environment variables.

Testing the Connection

1. **UI:** After saving, the Airflow Connections list should show your new connection as active.
2. **Code:** Write a simple Python DAG with a task using the `ElasticsearchPython` client. Attempt a simple operation like indexing a test document.

Troubleshooting Tips

- **Double-Check Fields:** Typos in the hostname, port, or credentials are common culprits.
- **Firewalls:** Ensure your Airflow environment has network access to your Elasticsearch cluster.
- **Logs:** Airflow logs often reveal the root cause of connection errors.

Additional Considerations

- **Multiple Clusters:** You can define connections to different Elasticsearch clusters if needed. Choose the relevant Conn Id in your DAGs.
- **Custom Certificates:** If using self-signed certificates, you'll need to provide the relevant certificate information to Airflow.

Resources

- **Airflow Documentation: Elasticsearch Connection** ([invalid URL removed])
- **Elasticsearch Security Documentation:** ([invalid URL removed])

Ready to Connect

With your connection in place, we're ready to build the heart of our Elasticsearch integration – the powerful `ElasticHook`. Let's dive in!

ElasticHook Essentials: Implementing the ElasticHook

In the previous chapters, we configured Elasticsearch and established a connection within Airflow. Now, we build the bridge that gives your Airflow DAGs seamless access to all that Elasticsearch offers.

The Purpose of the ElasticHook

Think of the ElasticHook as your specialized toolkit for interacting with Elasticsearch from within Airflow. Its core responsibilities include:

- **Establishing Connections:** It leverages the connection configuration you defined in Airflow.
- **Executing Queries:** Sending search requests, indexing documents, creating indices... the hook handles the communication with Elasticsearch.
- **Managing Responses:** It structures and returns data from Elasticsearch in a format Airflow understands.

Building Your ElasticHook

1. Setting up the Foundation

- **Import BaseHook:** Your ElasticHook will inherit from Airflow's BaseHook.
- **Utilize the Python Client:** Import the Elasticsearch library from the elasticsearch package (this is how we'll talk to Elasticsearch).

2. The __init__() Method

```python
from airflow.hooks.base import BaseHook
from elasticsearch import Elasticsearch

class ElasticHook(BaseHook):
    def __init__(self, conn_id='elasticsearch_default', *args, **kwargs):
        super().__init__(*args, **kwargs)
        self.conn_id = conn_id
        self.es = None  # Placeholder for our Elasticsearch client

        # Other methods to follow...
```

- **conn_id:** We'll use Airflow's connection functionality to retrieve the details we configured earlier.

3. Getting Connected: The get_conn() Method

```
def get_conn(self):
    if not self.es:
        conn = self.get_connection(self.conn_id)   # Airflow connection magic!
        conn_config = {}
        conn_config["host"] = conn.host
        if conn.port:
            conn_config["port"] = conn.port
        if conn.login:
            conn_config["http_auth"] = (conn.login, conn.password)

        self.es = Elasticsearch(conn_config)

    return self.es
```

- **Airflow Connections:** get_connection() fetches your stored credentials.
- **Client Creation:** We create an Elasticsearch client object and store it.

4. Core Methods: Let's Add Functionality

Here's a few essential methods to illustrate the concepts:

```
def info(self):
    return self.get_conn().info()

def index_document(self, index, doc_type, body, doc_id=None):
    return self.get_conn().index(index=index, doc_type=doc_type, body=body, id=doc_id)

def search(self, index, body):
    return self.get_conn().search(index=index, body=body)
```

Important Considerations

- **Error Handling:** Implement robust error handling to catch issues with your Elasticsearch connection or queries.

- **Expand Your Toolkit:** Add a wide array of methods to support the breadth of tasks you want to perform on Elasticsearch (delete, update, create index, etc.).

Example Usage in a DAG

```python
from airflow.operators.python import PythonOperator

def log_cluster_info(**kwargs):
    hook = ElasticHook()
    print(hook.info())

with DAG(...) as dag:
    task_log_info = PythonOperator(
        task_id='log_es_info',
        python_callable=log_cluster_info,
    )
```

Additional Notes

- **Version Compatibility:** Ensure your `elasticsearch` library version aligns with your Elasticsearch server.
- **Explore the Library:** The `Elasticsearch` client offers extensive functionality: https://elasticsearch-py.readthedocs.io/en/v7.17.5/

Ready to Interact! With your `ElasticHook`, you can streamline log analysis, index metrics, and power search features within your Airflow workflows.

Plugin Integration: Incorporating ElasticHook into the Plugin Ecosystem

Now that we've built our `ElasticHook`, let's make it a core part of your plugin's functionality.

1. Integration Points

The most common ways to leverage your hook are:

- **Custom Operators:** Create Operators tailored to the Elasticsearch tasks you often perform. Example: `ElasticsearchLogSearchOperator`, `ElasticsearchIndexOperator`. The `ElasticHook` will be used inside these operators.
- **Custom Sensors:** (Less common) If you need to monitor the state of Elasticsearch, a custom Sensor could utilize the `ElasticHook`.

2. Within Operators: Example

Let's imagine a `ElasticsearchIndexOperator`. Here's how it might use your Hook:

```python
from airflow.operators.python import PythonOperator
from airflow.plugins_manager import AirflowPlugin
from airflow.providers.elasticsearch.hooks.elasticsearch import ElasticHook

class ElasticsearchIndexOperator(PythonOperator):
    def __init__(self, index: str, doc_type: str, body: dict, *args, **kwargs):
        super().__init__(*args, **kwargs)
        self.index = index
        self.doc_type = doc_type
        self.body = body

    def execute(self, context):
        hook = ElasticHook()
        hook.index_document(
            index=self.index,
            doc_type=self.doc_type,
            body=self.body
        )
```

```
class MyElasticsearchPlugin(AirflowPlugin):
    name = "my_elasticsearch_plugin"
    operators = [ElasticsearchIndexOperator]
```

3. The Power of Abstraction

By using the `ElasticHook` within your operators, you:

- **Centralize Elasticsearch Logic:** Avoid re-implementing connection and interaction code in every task.
- **Enhance Testability:** You can test the `ElasticHook` independently, giving confidence in your operator logic.
- **Improve Maintainability:** Changes to how your plugin interacts with Elasticsearch can be focused within the hook itself.

4. Structure and Discoverability

Remember these structural points:

- **Hook:** Your `ElasticHook` implementation likely lives in a file like `hooks/elasticsearch_hook.py`.
- **Operators:** Operators using the hook would be in a file like `operators/elasticsearch_operators.py`.
- **Plugin Class:** These files are part of your plugin package, and the `AirflowPlugin` class definition tells Airflow where to find your custom components.

Example DAG Using Your Operator

Now, Airflow users can leverage your operator!

```
from airflow import DAG
from my_elasticsearch_plugin.operators.elasticsearch_operators import ElasticsearchIndexOperator

with DAG(
    dag_id='example_elasticsearch_dag',
    # ... other DAG settings ...
) as dag:

    index_website_logs = ElasticsearchIndexOperator(
        task_id='index_logs',
        index='website_logs',
```

```
        doc_type='_doc',
        body={
            "timestamp": "{{ ds }}",
            "user_id": 12345,
            "page_visited": "/shop"
        }
    )
```

Additional Considerations

- **Error Handling:** Include robust error handling in your operators as well, surfacing problems from Elasticsearch to the Airflow UI.
- **Parameterization:** Allow your operators to be flexible (which index, which doc type, etc.)
- **Task Configuration:** Using templating in your operator lets the DAG author provide input dynamically.

Best Practices

- **Unit Tests:** Cover both your ElasticHook and your Operators. This will make your plugin rock-solid.
- **Documentation:** If you plan to share your plugin, clear documentation on usage is essential.

Let Your Plugin Work Its Magic! By integrating your hook, you've built reusable building blocks enhancing the interaction between your Airflow workflows and Elasticsearch.

Next Up

Let's see your integrated hook in action and demonstrate its full potential in a practical scenario!

Hook Harmony: Witnessing the ElasticHook in Action

We've built the foundation of interacting with Elasticsearch from Airflow. Now, we'll illustrate common patterns and the tangible benefits the `ElasticHook` brings to your pipelines.

Scenario: Log Analysis

Let's imagine this use case:

1. Your application generates a steady flow of log files.
2. A log shipping process collects and pushes these logs to Elasticsearch.
3. You want to use Airflow to:
    - Monitor the health of your log ingestion process.
    - Run analytics queries on the logs to derive application insights.

Example 1: Checking Document Count

DAG Task: A task to verify if a reasonable number of log documents have arrived within a recent timeframe.

```python
from airflow.operators.python import PythonOperator
from airflow.providers.elasticsearch.hooks.elasticsearch import ElasticHook

def verify_log_count(**context):
    hook = ElasticHook()
    result = hook.search(
        index='my-logs-*',
        body={
            "query": {
                "range": {
                    "timestamp": {
                        "gte": context['execution_date'] - timedelta(hours=1)
                    }
                }
            }
        }
    )

    expected_count = 5000  # Adjust as needed
    if result['hits']['total']['value'] < expected_count:
```

```
        raise ValueError("Log ingestion volume too low!")

with DAG(...) as dag:
    check_ingestion = PythonOperator(
        task_id='check_log_ingestion',
        python_callable=verify_log_count
    )
```

How the Hook Helps

- **Abstracts Interaction:** We don't write raw Elasticsearch REST API calls.
- **Error Handling:** The ElasticHook can centralize error handling and retries.
- **Focus on Logic:** Our task code cleanly expresses the intent of log count validation.

Example 2: Application Error Analysis

DAG Task: Search logs for errors, aggregate error types, and potentially send alerts.

```
def analyze_errors(**context):
    hook = ElasticHook()
    result = hook.search(
        index='my-logs-*',
        body={
            "query": {
                "match": { "level": "ERROR"}
            },
            "aggs": {
                "top_errors": {
                    "terms": {"field": "error_type.keyword"}
                }
            }
        }
    )

    top_errors = results['aggregations']['top_errors']['buckets']
    # ... logic to process and potentially alert based on top_errors

with DAG(...) as dag:
    error_analysis = PythonOperator(
        task_id='analyze_app_errors',
        python_callable=analyze_errors
```

Benefits

- **Search Power:** Leverages Elasticsearch's query and aggregation capabilities.
- **Flexibility:** Your analysis logic in the DAG can adapt as requirements evolve, all built upon the `ElasticHook`.

Additional Use Cases

Your `ElasticHook` isn't just for logs! Consider:

- **Metrics Tracking:** Index operational metrics from various systems into Elasticsearch, and build Airflow DAGs to visualize trends.
- **Search-Driven Workflows:** A task could query Elasticsearch; the results then influence the downstream steps in your DAG, powered by XComs or TaskGroups.

Remember

- **Index Design:** How you structure your documents in Elasticsearch influences the types of queries you can do efficiently.
- **Airflow for Orchestration:** Airflow excels at orchestrating the process; the heavy lifting of data analysis rests on Elasticsearch's shoulders.

Let's Recap

With the `ElasticHook` as your bridge, you've unlocked a world of possibilities for how your Airflow workflows interact with Elasticsearch.

Further Exploration

- **Elasticsearch Best Practices:** Learn about document mapping, sharding, etc., from Elasticsearch's documentation (https://www.elastic.co/guide/).

Conclusion

Throughout this book, we've unraveled the power of Apache Airflow. You've journeyed from fundamental concepts to the depths of its architecture, from building your maiden DAG to mastering advanced orchestration techniques. Let's recap the highlights that have brought you this far:

Foundations Laid

- **Airflow's Purpose:** You understand why Airflow is a cornerstone of modern data engineering – scheduling, monitoring, and gracefully handling the complex dance of pipelines.
- **The Anatomy of a DAG:** DAGs, tasks, operators, and their relationships are no longer a mystery; they are the vocabulary with which you express your workflows.
- **Embracing Best Practices:** Modularity, testing, and clear organization concepts have shaped your approach to DAG development

User Interface Mastery

- **Visual Navigation:** The Graph View, Tree View, Gantt charts… Airflow's UI holds few secrets, offering different insights into the pulse of your pipelines.
- **Troubleshooting Toolbelt:** You've learned to investigate logs, pinpoint bottlenecks, and ensure your workflows run smoothly.

Building Your First Pipeline

- **Data's Journey:** Ingesting from sources, transforming, ensuring quality, and storing results – you've orchestrated this end-to-end process.
- **Operators as Building Blocks:** Whether using built-in Operators or those from Providers, you harness the right tools for each step.
- **The Power of Connections and Hooks:** Databases, cloud services, specialized systems… Airflow bridges the gaps within your data environment.

Reaching New Heights – Advanced Techniques

- **Workflow Optimization:** SubDAGs, TaskGroups, and XComs have unlocked ways to streamline complex pipelines and enhance efficiency.
- **Control and Flexibility:** Branching, conditional execution, and dynamic behavior let you build workflows that adapt to real-world data conditions.
- **Scaling with Executors:** You grasped the capabilities of different executors, tailoring how Airflow tackles workload distribution.

The Plugin Frontier

- **Extending Functionality:** The plugin architecture opened up possibilities to integrate bespoke tools and logic seamlessly into your data workflows.
- **The ElasticHook in Action:** With your Elasticsearch integration, you've brought log analysis, search capabilities, and more directly into the realm of Airflow.

Remember, the Journey Evolves

Airflow is a vibrant and ever-growing project. Stay curious and connected with the community:

- **Explore New Providers:** As new technologies emerge, so will Airflow's ability to interact with them.
- **Best Practices Continue to Evolve:** Learn from the experiences of others, contribute your own findings, and advance the collective knowledge base.
- **Real-World Inspiration:** Seek out case studies, open-source projects, and blog posts to see how Airflow is utilized across industries.

The Power to Orchestrate

You now possess the knowledge to transform raw data into actionable insights. Whether your pipelines handle a few tasks or a vast network of dependencies, the principles you've learned will guide you in building reliable, maintainable, and scalable solutions.

Airflow is your conductor's baton. The data universe is your orchestra. It's time to create your symphony!

Additional Resources

- **Official Apache Airflow Documentation:** (https://airflow.apache.org/docs/)
- **Airflow Community:** Seek help, join discussions (https://airflow.apache.org/community/)
- **Awesome Airflow:** Curated resources (https://github.com/jghoman/awesome-apache-airflow)

Go Forth and Orchestrate!

Printed in Great Britain
by Amazon